I Attract What I Am

Transform Failure
Into An
Orgasmically
Joyful Life & Business

Endorsements for *I Attract What I Am*:

"In the book, *I Attract What I Am*, Melissa Dawn eloquently describes her life story and the simple yet profound lessons she has learned through these life experiences. Most people, both men and women, will be able to relate to these experiences. Through her story she describes how we can navigate our life towards our dreams while managing career, relationships, children and that pesky inner dialogue.

Why re-invent the wheel and go through the same challenges when we can learn valuable lessons from Melissa's life story of transitioning from a corporate job to a successful entrepreneur, and at the same time finding meaningful and fulfilling relationships that help us grow spiritually and emotionally."

— Michael Allenbright,
  CEO, iZone Energy

"Life lessons are the best teaching tool that exists. Through her book, *I Attract What I Am*, Melissa Dawn, with skill and integrity through her instinctual journey brings to light, the golden treasures within life. In doing so, she teaches and helps you discover and adorn your inner miraculous self."

— Doreen Mary Bray,
  The Walking Sage

Endorsements for *I Attract What I Am*:

"Most books will change the way you think about life. This one will change your life."

— **Tarek Riman,**
  Founder & CEO of CapTaiM and Montrealtips.com

"Melissa weaves her personal story with her insights and revelations in an entertaining and enlightening way. Her commitment to her own journey shines through in the ways that she's able to be of service to others. I certainly believe that by embracing the important questions that she asks, someone would be able to transform their own lives into one of meaning, fulfillment, and fun."

— **John Germain Leto,**
  Business Coach and Shaman
  John & Eden

I Attract What I Am

Transform Failure
Into An
Orgasmically
Joyful Life & Business

By

Melissa Dawn

Published by
CEO OF YOUR LIFE
www.ceoofyour.life

I Attract What I Am
Transform Failure into an Orgasmically Joyful Life and Business©

Registration No. 1137172
Canadian Intellectual Property Office | An Agency of Industry Canada
© Copyright 2017 by Melissa Dawn

DISCLAIMER

Cover photos by Tarek Riman of Captaim.com
Front Cover Design by Nancy Morris
Cover Wrap by Steve Walters
Author photos by Isabelle Vaillancourt - StudioIV

First Printing, 2017

ISBN-13: 978-1542999922
ISBN-10: 1542999928

Table of Contents

Introduction - My Story

Spring of 2011:

I had just divorced – for the second time. And now, I was a single mom too. I didn't know how to be alone having gone from the house I grew up in to a marriage, to another marriage and here I was; single mom with primary custody to a four-year-old son, a house to maintain, training a new puppy and a job that was choking me. Quite frankly, I was terrified. I needed to work on every aspect of my life but what to do and where was I to start?

I needed help and I needed to learn how to ask for it. I started seeing a therapist to deal with my past issues and a life coach to help me work towards the life I wanted to create. What I knew was this; I dated emotionally unavailable men and took jobs where I was subordinated. In both my personal and professional lives I gave too much of myself away with little return. I felt I had to adapt who I was to please others. I felt I could not be accepted for being truly me. I was joyful and inspiring to people on the outside, yet on the inside I just didn't know who I was and what I truly wanted. It seems, I was discovering, that I didn't feel worthy of true success. On my own terms.

April 2013:

Two years later: The personal work I was doing was starting to generate some results. I was studying to become a healing practitioner, and I knew I wanted to become a certified coach and have my own coaching business. I was clear about what I wanted in my career, yet when it came to men, my confidence and self-esteem was decreasing by the minute. I accepted things I knew I shouldn't. I didn't tell anyone around me what I was going through because I knew the advice they would give me, and I didn't feel strong enough to act on it. A man I had been dating for a year and a half left me. I was devastated. Now I realize it was the best thing that could have happened. There's an expression, "with every breakdown there's a breakthrough" and that's what was happening with me.

I forged ahead with my dream to be a Certified Co-Active Coach and received my coaching certification, giving me the tools to ask powerful questions in order to guide the coachee to a path that is truly right for him or her. Funny, I went to coaching school with the intention of becoming certified but during this journey, I got so much more out of it. I became acquainted with myself. I identified my core values, my life purpose, what I truly wanted and what was important to me. I then launched a successful coaching business all while being a single mom. I was able to replace my salary as Vice President of Marketing within less than six months of leaving my day job. Career-wise, I felt great but with men, I was still accepting things I should not have been accepting.

April 2015:

After more therapy, coaching, energy work, meditation and connecting to my heart, I finally started to realize my true value as a woman in a relationship. I understood that what happens on the outside is a reflection of what is happening on inside. Now that I knew and valued myself, I finally attracted a relationship where I could let my guard down and be loved for who I was. I had successfully transitioned from my marketing job to a life & business coach & motivational speaker.

I'm sharing my journey with you in this book to show you that everything is possible when you choose the life you want. The power is in your hands (and your mind, your beliefs and your actions!) You and you alone can know what you want, and when it comes from your heart, all you need to do is take consistent steps towards your goals every single day. You are responsible for what you attract. You are the CEO of your life so go on, attract what you want!

I have created coaching programs based on my work and life experiences to help people build the kind of lives, careers and businesses they love waking up to – that they live in profound orgasmic joy! ☺

Chapter 1

Husband #1

It was the Spring of 2011. I had just gone through my second divorce. Yes, my second one.

My first divorce happened a little more than 10 years ago. I married my high school sweetheart and truthfully; neither of us were ready for it. We both came from strict religious backgrounds where dating for a long period of time wasn't acceptable, so at 18-years-old, we got married. I walked down the aisle feeling pretty sure I was making a mistake. My heart pumped loudly, silently telling me I should "RUN". I really wanted to. I remember glancing at the door to leave but with more than 200 people smiling up at me I chickened out and remained at the altar. I took those vows. Instead of listening to my heart, I let my fear lead me into the arms of a man I wasn't ready to marry, heeding the worry, "what will people think if I back out now?"

It didn't take long to see that my inner voice had been guiding me in the right direction. It was an unhappy union from the beginning. It's one thing to date someone and another thing to live with them, and I was only 18-years-old. What could I have known about being in a long-term relationship? We were worlds apart in how we approached life. We had a lot of growing up to do. We had different values. We had different ambitions. I knew our marriage wasn't going to make it into "happily ever after" and yet I stuck it out for eight years. Eight years of; what will people think, what will people say, how will I tell my parents for whom divorce is not an option, they'll never understand, I'm such a failure, what will I do on my own…?

For 8 years I was the "good wife" working at the marriage, by supporting him in all his pursuits and making sure when he came home that the house was clean, the table was set, the dinner was served and the social calendar was filled. I supported him in getting his university degree and while he launched his career and listened to all his work stressors while keeping his morale and motivation up. I suffered and sacrificed and although I was still in my twenties, I felt like a tired old woman. I lost my spark. I gave all that I could I give. I was miserable.

The only thing that kept me going was my career. I was always very ambitious. I got my Bachelor's Degree in Commerce and I started working for a multinational company. I loved what I was learning and the people I was working with.

One day, an employee of mine, Maria, commented on how exhausted I had become at the end of a 12-hour day. I remember thinking, "Funny, I'm more exhausted by the thought of going home to my husband than to continue working." Anyways, on this particular day, she placed a book in my hands and said, "Here. You should read this." She smiled and left. I looked at the book titled "Conversations with God" by Neale Donald Walsch and shuddered, "a book about conversations with God? This is exactly what I don't need." Because of my religious upbringing, I felt this book was last thing I wanted; religious orders on how to live my life.

A few weeks passed, and I did not open the book. Maria kept asking me about it and I simply said I did not have time to start reading it. Then one day my husband showed up at work. My body tensed, and I started to stress as he came through the door.

Maria could see the conversation I was having with him and how it was draining me. After he left, she came up to me and said, "Melissa, I know I am just your employee and I have no business in your personal life. I see you are a wonderful person and I see how much this relationship is draining you. Please read the book I gave you, I promise it will help you." Little did she know that the awakening of my spiritual journey was sparked as a result of her urging.

I decided to listen to her and read it. Wow. The book is written as a dialogue between Walsch, who was in a very low period of his life, and God. It's full of beautiful insights and life lessons and many surprising answers. I devoured the book and the other two in the series and took much of the wisdom from within those pages to heart. God wants us to be happy. And we need to do what makes us truly happy, no matter what others say or do.

It was then that I understood I couldn't just 'want' change, I had to 'choose' it. I started asking myself some questions. What do I truly want? What is important to me? I knew I had to leave my husband. I knew he was not bringing out the best in me. How was I to do it?

I also had another passion: to work overseas. As a child I dreamt of working on planes and traveling the world. I actually had created an album of every single city and country I wanted to visit. And then it came to me.

Bingo! I would apply for an overseas job!

I would leave my husband under the pretense that our separation was due to the long-distance career I chose. This way, it would be easier for him and my family to digest and then when I would ask for a divorce, it would not be surprising to anyone.

Okay, 20 years later, I realize this was not the best move. I should have just been upfront and left. But in my twenties, that was the best I could do.

I accepted a contract doing marketing and sales for a travel company in Cancun, Mexico. Cancun…need I say more? I was finally living my dream. I was living and working in a tropical country… without my husband! Because I was dealing with the public, I was treated like VIP everywhere I went. Bars and restaurants wanted to please me so, I could send clients their way. I enjoyed all the attention. I was living a dream. I felt myself come back to life. How could it possibly get better than this?

With my juices flowing again, exhilarated with what I was doing I gained the confidence to go forward with my divorce. I went back home a few months later and asked for a divorce. Still not courageous enough to be completely honest about it I told him that if we were meant to be, we could always get married again because then it would be because we really wanted to, not because society was forcing us to. I felt this was a softer way to deliver the message.

I was blessed that most of my friends understood and encouraged me to follow my dreams. The paperwork was done and I returned to Mexico. I worked in Cancun and then Puerto Vallarta – good times. I worked hard and I had a lot of fun too. I was living out the youth I felt I had missed being married so young.

I loved exploring new cultures, new ways of being, all kinds of spicy food and meeting really genuinely kind people. I can't tell you how happy I was. I would say orgasmically joyful in the sense of loving life and having fun. I was just enjoying my new-found freedom.

COACHING TIP: Always listen to your inner voice – especially when it's screaming. If you ignore that voice, the Universe will challenge you with harder and harder trials until you start listening.

Chapter 2

Husband #2

Two years later, I was transferred to Varadero, Cuba. Now this was a whole different vibe from Cancun. There was hardly any night life. The 24-hour Walmart and movie theaters were nonexistent. You were lucky to find even the most basic ingredients in a grocery store. The up-side of being in a country where there is not much is that people have mastered the art of charm and seduction. After all, there is not that much else to do. So, it was there and then that I fell for a Cuban. He was charming, he knew the words I wanted to hear, and he showed me a new perspective on life that I never learned living in a First World country. Through this experience, I learned to appreciate the day to day – simple things such as going to a grocery store and finding food you are looking for. In Cuba, you could never plan a meal; you had to cook based on what was available in the grocery store. I learned a lot. I became more down to earth. But, after two years in Cuba, I felt I had enough of the "Cuban experience." I was missing the "civilized" world.

In Cuba everything was an adventure. If you went to visit a friend, you never knew if you would make it there or home again, because the bus might or might not show up.

I wanted to leave Cuba but I didn't want to leave my boyfriend behind and the only way to get my boyfriend to come with me to Canada was to marry him. I wasn't ready to get married again, but there was truly no other way.

We signed our papers in front of a Cuban lawyer and were married. The paperwork to bring him to Canada was quite a challenge. I was doing the papers from Canada while he was in Cuba. It took over a year, but then at last he came to Canada as a permanent resident. I thought, "YES! Finally! Our lives together can begin and we can create our happy ever after."

Hmmm…. not so fast Melissa. Him coming to Canada was like dating a completely different person. We went from living in a hotel where everything was taken care of for us to having the reality of paying the rent, cooking and cleaning. It was a whole different reality. In Cuba, he had worked as a representative and was quite sociable, which was one of the things I loved most about him. But once in Canada, it was almost like the cold weather had made him cold. We didn't socialize much and when I asked him why he said: "When I was in Cuba I had to socialize to make money. Here, I don't have to. I would much rather keep to myself." That was an eye-opener. I didn't see this coming. Me, a social bee, living with someone who didn't care to socialize. Red flag! With time, more and more red flags came up but I let them rest I decided to be positive and trust that things would work out. We decided to start a family. It took about two years to get pregnant. I learned along the way that I had a tumor on my pituitary gland that was preventing conception. Once it was diagnosed and treated, I decided I was going to get pregnant right away. And I acted as if it was true. We painted a baby's room, got the right furniture along with some baby toys –and guess what? I got pregnant the same week. Yay! I was so happy.

Everything to this point had been a struggle. To be in Cuba was a struggle, to bring him to Canada was a struggle, to get pregnant was a struggle. And I acted as if it was true. Looking back on that time, I now realize that it was the Universe's way of telling me this was not the right path. When the path is meant for you, it comes to you with ease. This was definitely not the case in this relationship. I did not heed the Universe's warnings…I was still choosing to move forward on positive mindset. Reflecting back, I ask myself why I settled. Why did I not heed the warnings? Today I could say that it was because I lacked confidence. I didn't think I could find better. I believed I was flawed so I thought I'd never find someone who could love me just as I was.

I had a so-so pregnancy. I didn't feel like my husband really understood how I felt. I didn't feel I was getting the support I needed. I tried to voice it, but either I wasn't expressing myself properly or he chose not to hear what I was saying – or maybe a bit of both. My son came into this world in August, 2006. I actually had the honor of pulling him out of me. What a beautiful moment. He came out a strong, determined baby with his eyes wide open looking straight at me. What a beautiful day. What a beautiful new beginning. I was blessed with an angel. Now, I thought to myself, "this is my happy ever after. We have a baby together." Wrong again.

Our son represented the beginning of the end of our relationship. It was so important to me to be a good mother. I poured every ounce of my energy into my son. Like most new moms, I didn't sleep, and I lost myself in "mommyland."

I pretty much knew the relationship was over by the time my son was a few months old. I nevertheless continued the relationship, for all the wrong reasons.

Wow! I was still afraid of what people would think. Here I was considering divorce #2. I "imported" my ex-husband from Cuba and I felt a lot of guilt around leaving him alone in Canada. My son would be growing up in a one parent home. The gremlins – those voices of "reason" that reject change and hold us back from moving forward into a life we truly want - were having a field day. The Universe gave me several signs, those red flags I kept ignoring, that this was not the man I was meant to build my life with and I didn't listen. So the Universe made this break-up happen for me. Now I was single and I had a four-year-old son.

COACHING TIP: When something or someone you want is a constant struggle to get, it's the Universe telling you it's not meant for you.

Chapter 3

Hitting Gremlin Rock Bottom

I was so ashamed. A second divorce, really? What did that say about me? Who would want me after that? Was I just horrible at relationships? What was I good at? This marriage gave me a structure: family life, kids, retirement. Now what? The structure was broken. What was next?

So how could it get even worse than becoming a single mom with a four-year-old? Easy for me, apparently! I loved everything about my job working in marketing for an online company. I loved the people I worked with and enjoyed a great relationship with my boss – perhaps too good. We shared a lot and joked around a lot. We were both going through some struggles and supported each other. Unfortunately, this made his girlfriend uncomfortable and she gave him an ultimatum: fire me or she would leave him. (And no, we didn't sleep together.) Guess what he chose? We had a conversation and he told me he had to let me go. He was nice about it and let me take my time until I found something else. So now, on top of everything else, I needed to find a new job. Talk about a year of challenges. The Universe has a funny way of getting me to listen. First it sends up red flags and challenges me until I tune in and then it takes care of me.

I got two great job offers, both more lucrative than my current position. I chose to become Vice President of Marketing in a tech startup. The Universe seemed to be supporting me and directing me on a new route. In order to help my four-year-old son transition from being with both parents to being mostly with me, I decided to get a puppy. I thought this was a great way to distract him from what was really going on. He had always wanted a puppy. New life, new job, a new puppy – what was next?

I needed help. I didn't want to repeat the same mistakes. I was doing things on autopilot, living in survival mode. Having been married at the tender young age of 18, I didn't truly know who I was or what my greater purpose could be. Be a single mom, train a new puppy, start a new job, deal with an ex. Yes, I was busy…but there had to be more to life than this. Why did it all happen? "OK Universe, what are you telling me and what are you steering me towards. I'm here. I'm listening. I'm ready to figure my life out."

I decided to take my life to the next level. I made one of the most important decisions and investments ever: I hired a life coach. Her name was Meisha Rouser. Little did she know the tremendous impact she would have on my life.

Oh, side note: soon after I started my new job, my former boss's girlfriend left him – he had let go of me to keep her and she left him. I had no idea why this happened, but I knew there was something much bigger in store for me. I decided to find out.

COACHING TIP: When you hit rock bottom and you consciously decide to make changes that feel good, the Universe supports you by propelling you forward.

I Attract What I Am · *Melissa Dawn*

Chapter 4
The Debut of "Future Me"

Meisha, my life coach, asked me all kinds of questions that I had never before asked myself. She recommended exercises that I thought were pretty "out there" – but I was so ready for something more and I knew I had to do things differently so I was completely open to what she was recommending. Our first session began with her bringing me five years ahead and visualizing "future me"... what my heart truly desired. I saw myself madly in love (for real this time), living in a beautiful home with another child and a big German Shepherd. I saw myself with my own business, my own brand, with lots of people supporting me. I saw myself traveling and having a great work life balance. Was this just a dream? Was this possible? Was this just me being ridiculous?

My coach told me whenever I got discouraged to connect to the me of the future and ask her for advice. She told me to become like a magnet to my future self; to envision me as my future self now so I could attract all the energies that would bring me to that place.

At this point I had been separated for six months with already a few coaching sessions under my belt. I was also working with an amazing therapist who used different energetic techniques to heal. Her name was Marie-Danielle Boyer. She helped me deal with my emotions and fears that came up as I was settling into the role of single mom with a new puppy. I started to feel a little lighter. I was ready to open myself up to new experiences. My co-workers and friends kept telling me to go out and start dating again. I wanted to, but I was afraid. What would dating be like after being in a 10-year relationship? Would I even know what to do? How would being with someone else be? How would kissing someone else be? I was a super sociable person. I was successful at what I did. Yet when it came to men, I had zero confidence. I decided to take a step towards facing my fears. One of my friends kept raving about a dating coach so I decided to invest in her online program to build my confidence up.

I listened to one of her programs with more than 20 hours of online advice. I read her material; I did the exercises. None of her advice aligned with me or my values. One piece of advice; always date three men at a time so you don't give off a vibe of being needy or waiting. Uh… no. Not my style at all and not something I was willing to do.

Her logic was that if you're dating three people, you're not dwelling on one man getting back to you. You're busy and not desperate, and she says this is sexy to a man. Was I so out of the dating game? Had things changed that much? Or was I just different? I thought… well, she's the dating coach expert; she's in a successful relationship, she has thousands of people raving about her program, she must know something I don't know.

COACHING TIPS: Need to make a tough decision? Ask yourself, "What would "the me" of my ideal future decide?"

When you want something to be different in life, you have to be ready to do something different.

Chapter 5

Mismatch.com

I decided to start meeting men again. I started by putting my profile on a popular dating site and was inundated with messages. Wow. All these men wanted to get to know me? I showed a friend of mine the guys who were interested and she said, "Go for this one. He's handsome." He looked like a player to me, but I said, why not…and I messaged him. He was French Canadian with a good job. We exchanged a few emails. He seemed intelligent and friendly, so I agreed to meet him for lunch. I was so nervous as this was my first date in many years that I even considered cancelling it but then I told myself to look at it as a business meeting and I went through with it.

He did look like his picture. We sat down and were given menus. Oh my, I did not want to look like a klutz (did I mention I am a bit of a klutz?) or smell like garlic or commit a faux pas. He told me he had only been on the site for two weeks and had four dates so far but never any second dates and I told him this was my first date and that I was super nervous. Ten years ago men were interested in me, but now, as a single mom, how would I rate? So much pressure! He had ordered sausages for both of us, it arrived and of course, klutz that I am, a piece flew off my plate as I tried to slice into it. I was embarrassed but he laughed and said, "You are really nervous, relax. You're the best first date I've had." Me? I was so flattered. We parted ways, I went back to work and within twenty minutes my first date texted me to say he had a great time and wanted to do it again. Wow. Dating is easy, I thought. I can do this. What's everyone complaining about?

We had a second lunch-time date and it was on my birthday! I remember it was a Friday. He texted me numerous times all afternoon and into the evening. Then the texts stopped; nothing on Saturday, nothing on Sunday, nothing on Monday. I was confused…what had happened? I started to doubt myself and then remembered the dating coach's advice that I didn't take: "Always date three and keep the focus on me." So I checked my messages on the dating site but there was no person of interest.

He finally texted me back four days later. Okay, maybe this was normal…after all, we weren't in a relationship. He invited me for supper on a Thursday night. It felt good to be with a man and have good conversations. We went for a walk. He tried to hold my hand but I kept walking faster so he couldn't get close to me. I just wasn't ready. I had only been with two men and I had been married to both of them! I was afraid of not being perfect. This fear paralyzed me on the date. He drove me home and he tried to kiss me at the doorstep. As soon as his lips got close to mine, I froze. My ex-husband's face appeared in my head. I felt I was cheating. I just could not make my lips move.

I knew I had to do something about my freezing up. Why was I so scared? I decided to get help and booked an appointment with Marie-Danielle. That turned out to be a great idea. I don't quite remember what she did or said, I just remember coming out of that session feeling super light. Now I was on a mission to have my first post-divorce kiss.

I didn't hear from him over the weekend. I wrote to him but got no reply. I called him, no answer. I finally heard from him almost a week later. He said he'd been busy and we arranged to have another lunch date a week later. In two weeks he did not have time for me? Okay, so maybe dating wasn't so easy.

The date finally came up – I was excited to see him again but right away he told me he had accepted a position in Quebec City which was three-and-a-half hours away. He didn't feel we should be officially dating and that I was welcome to visit. He walked me back to the office and tried to kiss me but I was uncomfortable as we were in front of my office building. I felt it was unprofessional. So again, I froze. I think the Universe and I were getting to know each other a little better because I'm pretty sure the Universe was letting me know this was not my happy ever after. Indeed, it was the last time we saw each other.

This online dating thing was not for me. I went home and removed myself from the dating site, never to return to it. I was still first kiss-less but was OK with it. The Universe has my back!

COACHING TIPS: Do not listen to what the "experts" tell you. If something feels wrong, it probably is. Always trust your inner voice.

Chapter 6

The Doctor

One of my friends, Asmaa, had been encouraging me for a while to try speed dating. I knew a few people who had tried it, but I never heard of any made-in-heaven matches that came from it. I decided to give it a try. Why not? I'll go with my girlfriend and we'll have fun whether we meet someone interesting or not. We signed up for a University Graduates Speed Dating event. Figuring that at least the men here will be educated.

I remember it well. It was December 22nd and pouring rain. We drove around, got lost and parked far from the entrance and when we arrived, we were soaked. Our hair was matted and messy and make-up stained our faces. Oh well, if a guy was meant to be, he was meant to be whether we looked our best or not. The way speed dating works is the woman stays seated in her seat and the men take turns going from table to table, with only seven minutes to speak. I had interesting conversations with the first few but the next two men made the seven minutes feel like hours. I couldn't wait for the bong to indicate they had to move over to the next table.

Then a man with dark hair and green eyes ended up in front of me. He was a Doctor. There was some chemistry. I must admit talking with him made me feel a spark inside, a feeling I had not felt in years.

I spoke with a few men at this event. At the end, everyone was asked to put a checkmark beside the name or names of the people they'd like to see again. Mutual matches receive an email the next day with contact information. I had now met a few new men and I had to choose which ones I actually wanted to date. I found this a bit difficult because I would have liked to keep in touch with a few as friends. But I didn't want to give out the wrong intentions and so I decided to only check off The Doctor (in my mind, that's what I called him). I waited impatiently for the email which would let me know if The Doctor wanted to see me too. It was supposed to arrive 24 hours later but there was some sort of glitch and I had to wait 72 hours to find out. I received a notice saying he did. I was so flattered. I waited. Would The Doctor contact me? I didn't want to make the first move. Christmas came and went. New Year's Day came and went. I figured if he had been interested, he would have contacted me by now. I was disappointed. Then on January 6, I received an email from him, saying he had been travelling overseas to visit his family. As well, he had just moved into a new home and that was why he had not written me sooner.

Fair enough. We started writing to each other. Truthfully the messages were okay, not overly exciting.

We had been communicating for a bit over a week and I was thinking that if he does not ask me out soon, I'll just give up. Funny, he asked me out just a few hours later. Yes! He asked me out for that very night. I remembered the dating coach saying not to accept last-minute dates because you don't want to look like you don't have a life or other options. I contemplated that but it was a Saturday night, my son was with his Dad, and the next available time without my son would be in two weeks. I went against the dating coach's advice and accepted the date.

I dressed up. This was going to be an exciting date. And guess what? He lived only a few blocks away – we were practically neighbors. We decided to meet in a local restaurant club. As I was driving to meet him, I made up my mind that this would be the night I'd have my first post-divorce kiss, no matter what. Whether I saw a second date coming or not, I had to get over my fear. I arrived at the restaurant and looked for him. Truthfully, I could not remember exactly what he looked like but all of a sudden he came up to me with a big smile and kissed me on both cheeks. I was happy to see him. The restaurant was jam-packed, and he took my hand and led me through the crowd. I felt at ease with him. We went upstairs for drinks. Actually, he did not drink. He just ordered orange juice. I was stressed about the date, so I went for a vodka tonic. He paid. According to the dating coach, he was doing everything right.

I decided to come right out and be totally honest about everything – how I was a single mom and how I was a bit stressed about dating. I felt I'd rather be straight up about myself and my situation than to put on a front. He was okay with everything. I liked that. We talked about his trip, our families, and our friends.

We talked for hours, the time just flew by and then he asked me to dance. Dance? Oh my…I had not danced in years. I had taken salsa and merengue lessons about ten years earlier but I was rusty and as you now know, a bit of a klutz. He showed off his salsa skills and I must admit they were not bad. I felt a bit stiff but decided to at least try to loosen up and dance. I was looking at his feet to follow, ensuring my steps were following his when he lifted my chin up and brushed his lips on mine. I didn't see it coming. I froze for a few seconds and then I said to myself: "Respond…you can do this…kiss him back." It felt a bit unnatural and I was nervous as hell, but I was facing my fear. I was so proud of myself – I had my first post-divorce kiss!

Later, when we said good-bye he hugged me and said he would call. I hoped he would but did not want to set myself up for disappointment, so I told myself not to expect a call.

Believe it or not, he texted me the very next day and said he wanted to come over to my place. I was flattered The thing was, I had my son. I wasn't sure how to reply. Truthfully, I was tired and I didn't feel comfortable with him coming over when my son was there. For all I knew, he could still be a psychopath. Why would I put my son in an unsafe situation? I told him he could come over in a few days. We had several dates and they all went well. Sometimes I didn't hear from him for a few days but I told myself we were not yet in a committed relationship, so I should have zero expectations. We had been dating for about two months when he told me his mom was coming to visit from overseas and he would not be able to see me as much because she would not approve of him seeing someone who was not from the same culture and religious background. I felt a red flag go up but decided to ignore it. Can you believe it? I was still ignoring red flags when it came to my love life!

His mom stayed here for about three months and during that time he would basically come see me when his mom was asleep and return home before she woke up. Imagine, we were both in our 30s, professionals making over $100K each and acting like teenagers, hiding from our parents.

I began to question all of it. Should I stay in this relationship? Is there any hope of anything long-term if he is hiding this relationship from his mom? I questioned him straight out: "I am not asking you to commit, I know we have just been seeing each other for a few months. But I need to know if there is any chance this relationship can be long-term or is this just a fun pastime for you?" His reply was: "If God wants it to be, it will be." I agreed. I ignored all the red flags. My friends advised me to leave him. They told me men like this either find someone from their own culture to marry or they expect you to convert to theirs. I decided this was a chance I had to take. I did not feel 100 per cent comfortable in the relationship, but I was enjoying his company.

COACHING TIP: Never ever ignore the red flags. They're put there for you as signs from the Universe.

Chapter 7

The Crash

I loved my new VP Marketing job and I was making progress in other areas of my life working with my life coach. I was working out more, eating better, sleeping better and feeling happier inside. I admired how my coach was helping me. I aspired to be like her, I wanted to have this kind of impact on people. When I asked her how she became a certified coach, she told me she had studied at The Coaches Training Institute which is considered the Harvard in coaching, I looked into it but it was out of reach for me at the time; a one-year intensive program at a cost of $10, 000 U.S. for which I didn't have the time or resources.

I decided to take another route to help people. I decided to become a healer. I took a few energy courses in the Theta healing technique, a meditation technique and spiritual philosophy with the purpose of getting closer to the Creator - not specific to one religion but accepting them all. It's a training method for your mind, body and spirit that allows you to clear limiting beliefs and live life with positive thoughts. I also took courses in Access Consciousness, which consists of life-changing techniques, tools and processes designed to empower you to create the life you truly desire. In my first Theta healing class, we were shown a healing technique which we then practiced on our classmates. It was my very first time doing any type of healing and on my first try, I released a woman of 30 years of hurt caused by sexual abuse from her father. She let out a huge scream and all her frustrations came out.

She cried and thanked me profusely for freeing her from this heavy pain. I must admit I was shocked. I couldn't believe what had just happened. In that moment I knew without a doubt that I was meant to be a healer. My teacher looked at me and said, "I have been doing this for years and I never had such an intense healing experience that you just had. You are in the right place."

I started doing energy work on close friends and family. I really enjoyed it and people did see shifts. For instance, one of my friends who had unsuccessfully tried to quit smoking for years was finally able to break the habit through my energy sessions. I also had friends who went from being in severe debt to financial abundance. I definitely had a gift. But when I talked about what I did outside my close circle of friends and family, people thought I was losing it. How could a VP of Marketing be doing all this woo-woo stuff? I tried talking about my energy work more openly in order to get more clients, but I felt people looked at me like I was crazy and I was insecure about it. I did not have the confidence at the time to stand up for what I truly believed. I let my gremlins take over and stopped trying to get new clients for energy work, limiting it to friends and family.

I continued to see The Doctor. We had some good times; we shared a lot of laughs. Yet there was always something that prevented the relationship from moving forward. Either his mom and dad were in town and we had to revert to hiding our relationship, or he travelled for work, or he travelled for a month or more to his hometown. I was always waiting for the ball to drop. We had booked a trip to Costa Rica for my friends' wedding. I was really looking forward to that. About six weeks before the trip, he called and texted less and less often. Then on Easter Friday, sure enough, the ball dropped. He came by to tell me he had met a girl from the same culture and religion so he could not see me in the context of a relationship anymore. He said we could still be friends that we could still go to Costa Rica together. Although I was always on edge that it would come to this, it still hurt like hell. I knew he had feelings for me. I knew this was a cultural decision. I told him I could not stay in the same room with him in Costa Rica if he was with someone else. He said he was disappointed because he had already scheduled the time off, but that he understood. He left.

I cried so much. Pain took over my body. It was overwhelming. I loved him. I kept asking, how could this happen to me? I was so sad, so hurt and in so much pain that I could not even get out of bed the next morning. It was Easter weekend. I had to get up and feed my son and I just couldn't move. If it wasn't for my son, I would have not even made an attempt to move. I called Marie-Danielle, sobbing. She had such a good heart. She did some energy work on me, I felt a jolt in my heart and began to regain some strength, enough to pull myself out of bed and fix breakfast for my son. I'm forever grateful to her,

COACHING TIP: No matter how bad things seem, remember things are happening FOR you and not TO you.

Chapter 8

Opening Up to Something Larger

I had been through two divorces, I was a single mom, I had lived in foreign countries alone, but the pain I felt from this breakup superseded everything. I was not in love with my ex-husbands when the breakup happened – The Doctor was the guy I was in love with (or so I thought). I could not imagine meeting someone else who would make me feel this way again. Confidence? Shattered. Self-esteem? Zero. Happiness? What's that? I hardly ate or slept. Something had to change and that something had to be me. I had to give myself something to look forward to. That's when I decided to take the leap and sign up to become certified through The Coaches Training Institute. I didn't have the money, but I had to do it. I really wanted to change people's lives and I felt by being certified, I would earn credibility from professionals. The program was scheduled to start in July, just three months away.

The was only one other thing I was looking forward to, this wedding of my friends, Mariana and Jay, on a beach in Costa Rica. A lot of close friends would be there. I was counting the days until I took the flight.

I also wanted to take steps towards creating my coaching business. I started looking at what other coaches were doing, how they were marketing themselves and I started to create content based on what seemed successful out there – but with my own twist. I created business cards choosing yellow as the main color because it's a happy color and I took a picture of myself with a shovel digging in the ground to indicate that coaching meant digging deep into yourself. I was so proud of what I was doing. I was serious about creating a business as a coach. I started telling people what I was doing and soon got my first paying client. I was at my son's karate lesson, talking to other parents, when one of them came up to me and told me he needed a coach. Wow, that was that easy. I knew coaching aligned with my higher path and I felt the Universe was showing me this was the path I was destined to take.

It was time to go to Costa Rica. As much as I had been looking forward to it, I had mixed feelings. It made me sad that The Doctor wouldn't be there with me. I got on the plane and the seat beside me was empty; it would have been The Doctor's seat. I cried and cried. I did not understand why the relationship had to end. My heart still yearned for him. I arrived in Costa Rica and my friends greeted me happily at the airport. I felt loved. We got to the hotel, settled in our rooms and then went straight to the beach. I needed this. Ohhh, the sand on my feet was so healing and being surrounded by people who loved me was exactly what I needed to lift me higher.

More friends arrived from around the world throughout the day. Mariana, who was about to get married, introduced me to a friend of hers, from California. There was an immediate connection between us but I wasn't ready for anything, so from the beginning, I blurted out that I just had a bad breakup and didn't want to know anything about men. "No worries," he replied.

We had an incredible conversation, very spiritual. Our conversation was cut short as we greeted other arrivals. It was amazing to be in a hotel where almost everyone in the hotel is there for a friend's wedding. What a feeling. Everywhere I turned there was someone wonderful or a beautiful beach. How could it get better than this?

That night at supper I was eyeing Spiritual Man (that's what I called him) but I didn't want to approach him. I wasn't ready to be with someone else, yet at the same time, I was. He came to my table. We shared food. We laughed. He had a great sense of humor. OK... this was good. I was starting to feel something again. The next day we went zip-lining as a group in the jungle and to visit dormant volcanos. We also went tubing and painted our bodies with volcanic mud. I felt alive again and I was so grateful to my friends Mariana and Jay and for this trip.

The next day I woke to get some fresh coconut from a man selling juice on the beach. I enjoyed starting my morning drinking fresh juice and walking on the beach for a few kilometers. The view was breathtaking. The sand, the ocean, the energy Mother Nature was nourishing, healing and protecting me. As I was taking this morning's walk, I noticed Spiritual Man surfing. He came up to me and asked me to join him in the water but I found the water too cold so I said no. "I am telling you by the end of the week I will get you in the water," he said. I replied that I couldn't take the cold water "I bet you a hug you will," he replied." I laughed and agreed to the bet. Certain that he would lose. Funnily enough, later that day the sun became increasingly hot and my friends convinced me to go swimming with them. Of course, as I was swimming Spiritual Man passes by. "Ha, caught you – you owe me a hug." Part of me was excited to hug him and part of me was scared. I thought if it's meant to be, it will be.

The wedding was that afternoon. Mariana and Jay, had a spiritual wedding. Using the services of a Shaman couple, John Germain Leto and Eden Clark to perform the ceremony. I had never seen a Shaman observance and I absolutely loved it. They smudged everyone before entering the ceremony area. Smudging consists of taking sage and burning it and waving it under the soles of your feet and across your whole body to a bit above your head in order to remove any negative energy. This ensures you are coming into the wedding circle with the best of energies and intentions. How beautiful. It was all so peaceful and serene.

The ceremony was impressive from beginning to end. John opened a sacred space by calling in the four winds, Mother Earth and Father Sun. An overwhelming calmness came over me. I felt so connected with everyone at the ceremony. The vows were beautiful. They then passed around flowers and everyone thought of an intention and mentally put it into a flower for the couple. Taking the flowers, they mixed them with pure waters brought in from Peru and blessed them. I felt so many emotions during the rite. I also vowed to learn more about Shamans. Their message really resonated with me.

The reception followed. And it was beautiful. I decided to spend most of it taking care of Aqualine, John and Eden's two-month old daughter of, the Shamans who had performed the ceremony. Her energy was so beautiful. I enjoyed having her in my arms and her parents enjoyed spending some baby-free time at the wedding. At one point, Aqualine wanted her mom's milk and started sucking my arm so hard she actually gave me a hickey. I started to laugh and asked myself was this foreshadowing something to come?

I returned Aqualine to her parents and joined my friends on the dance floor. Spiritual Man came up and said we should get some drinks. We went to the bar but it was already closed. "Why don't we make our own?" Spiritual Man asked. I told him I had some vodka in my room. We got the bottle and managed to get some orange juice by paying some kitchen workers. We met my friends and Spiritual Man made drinks for all. He was kind, sweet, generous and nice to my friends. I felt he was one of my angels. I wonder, "did the Universe send him to me to rebuild my confidence and show me that good men exist and love is still possible?" Being with him made me realize that I definitely needed a man who was spiritual. I was spiritual, so my partner had to be too. I did not have this in any of my previous relationships and I realized it now had to be non-negotiable.

Spiritual Man and I went into a corner to talk. He looked at me and said, "If we lived in the same city, we would be in a relationship." I felt my body vibrate.

These words gave me confidence. Then he said, "Oh, and you owe me a hug." He came up to me and hugged me. It was sweet. As we hugged, my friends passed by and I got shy and pulled away. We then went off to the beach. The moon was luminous and large that night and so were the stars. We lay on the beach and talked and laughed for a long time. No one came. We had the moon, the stars and the beach to ourselves. I felt good.

Just then, many of our friends decided to show up and to take a night swim. We decided to leave. I felt it was time to go to my room. He asked me if I was okay and told me he hoped we could spend more time together. He walked me to my room, killed a cockroach in front of my door, hugged me and wished me a good night. I just could not believe this. I thanked the Universe. The Doctor had never treated me like this. All the tears I had cried over him, for what? The Universe was showing me that I should raise my standards because there was much better out there for me.

The next day, I booked my first Shamanic energy session with John Germain Leto. I had mixed emotions and no idea what to expect. I was feeling a bit guilty because although I had spent time with a new man, I was thinking of my ex. I shared my feelings with John. He told me it was best if I energetically cut ties with my ex in order to get rid of any remnants between us. That way, I would be able to move forward with my life with more ease. He explained to me when people come together in a relationship, cords are formed between the two hearts.

It's an energetic tunnel: information, emotions, feelings pass in that tunnel. The cords can strengthen over time. When the relationship is over and those cords are still there, people are unable to move on. People are attached energetically, so you need to cut the cords. When the cords are cut, it gives the person a greater ability to move on because they are not tethered to that person anymore. Sometimes you need to close the book on what was, so something new can be formed. He also explained that if a couple gets back together, new cords are formed.

I hesitated. I wasn't ready to cut the ties with The Doctor. I guess part of me still wanted to hold on to the possibility we could get back together. I had no idea why. Logically it did not make sense. But I guess healing is a process and it does not happen overnight. John did clear energies that were not serving me in order to help me step onto a higher path. I really enjoyed the session. I felt calm and confident. I could now go back and take my life to a new level. I promised myself I would only do things that felt right for me, that I would learn to honor my inner voice no matter what anyone told me.

I went for a long walk on the beach to absorb everything from the session. I felt I was resonating on a higher frequency and I made a vow to myself that I would always work towards becoming my best self and taking care of myself, not only on a physical but on an energetic level as well. My stomach started to feel a bit queasy. I decided to go back to my room; it seems I had gotten some type of tourista. It was my final evening in Costa Rica. I wanted to fully enjoy it, but my stomach was not allowing it. I went for supper with my friends. Spiritual Man and I talked but we both seemed to be feeling sick.

I went to get some water and bumped into Eden. She was beautiful, enlightened and well-spoken. I truly admired her. I wanted to become more like her. For some reason that night, perhaps because I was not feeling well, some pain from my breakup was resurfacing. I told her about it and she looked at me and told me straightforward: "Melissa, people leave your life in order for new people to come in. Embrace it. It's for your highest good." What a way to look at it. As simple as that. Did The Doctor leave for Spiritual Man to come in?

Just then, Spiritual Man passed by and said he was feeling lousy and was going to his room. He asked me to pass by so we could say good bye as we were both taking early flights back the next morning. About 30 minutes after he left, I too felt queasy. I passed by his room and hesitated to knock as I felt I might be really sick and preferred to be by myself. I gently knocked on his door but I think he didn't hear me. I went to my room to take care of myself. I hardly slept. I woke up early, packed my stuff and said my good-byes. Spiritual Man had left in the wee hours of the morning, so we never got to say goodbye. I was a bit sad about that. I got in a cab and made my way to the airport. And on the way, I thanked the Universe for this beautiful trip; how much it recharged me, how it helped me go on a new spiritual path, how I was surrounded by so much beauty in nature and good energy. I felt loved by so many people and most of all, I had faith that the Universe had my back and that better quality people and opportunities were entering my life. This trip was such a gift. I definitely understood that sometimes things had to end, but they were indeed so something better could come in.

COACHING TIP: The Universe truly does have your back. Trust that when one door closes, it's a sign that a new and better one is waiting to open for you.

I Attract What I Am · *Melissa Dawn*

Chapter 9

What Do I Want to Create?

I returned to Montreal from Costa Rica armed with a peaceful, calm and spiritual energy that I intended to hold onto. I messaged Spiritual Man and we agreed to keep in touch and see what the Universe had in store for us. I knew I had a business event in Vegas in a few months, so we agreed to meet then.

I started to get premonitions that a new man was on his way to me. One day at work, I had a premonition that I would meet the man of my life in this office and that he would be partly Brazilian. He would be smart, sexy and we would connect on physical, business, emotional and spiritual levels. The premonition presented me with what seemed to be the perfect man for me. I envisioned him tall, with dark hair and olive skin. The premonition lasted a few minutes and then disappeared. The vision was so clear I could feel him. His energy was soothing.

The first weekend of my life coaching certification program came and it was a weekend I will never ever forget. The course, Fundamentals, was aimed at getting an overview of what certification would be like and getting our coaching feet wet. From the first minute that I entered the room I knew this was the right decision. Beautiful energy, everyone excited and interested in getting to know each other and the most amazing instructors.

Throughout the weekend I kept getting goosebumps. I felt so many truths were spoken. Everything I was learning was aligned with who I was. Not only did I love all the coaching tools provided to me but I realized coaching was actually spiritual. Oh my, I had an epiphany that I could actually combine my two passions! I didn't have to deny my spiritual and energy work – I could combine them through life coaching. This was one of the best and most exciting realizations of my life. I was on cloud nine that weekend. We had to practice all the coaching tools we were learning amongst ourselves. We had many deep conversations which brought the group extremely close. By the end of the weekend we were all in love with each other and no one wanted to leave. I was sure that this was the beginning of a very, very exciting journey. I was still on cloud nine when I went to work Monday morning. Everyone noticed and asked if I had sex. Haha – I told them I had a coachingasm. I could not wait until the next coaching training weekend. Unfortunately, it was two months later. I was counting the days.

During this time, John Germain Leto and I kept in touch. He knew my passion for being a coach and offered to help me with branding. I wasn't sure how to interpret this. After all, I had about 20 years of marketing experience and I already had a rough draft of my website. I showed it to him. He said it was good on paper but it didn't represent who I truly am as a person. I was taken aback. But since he did help brand Beyoncé I decided to pay more attention to what he was saying. He said, your website is being conceived from the level of the mind but you need to convey a deeper message. "You need to connect your mind and heart and create your branding from that space." At that time, I had no idea what he was trying to say but I decided to heed his advice. We started having sessions and he guided me on how to let go of fixed visions. He taught me to stop feeling that I had to make all decisions on my own and carry the weight of the world on my shoulders. He taught me how to connect with my heart and go with the flow of life. As I was learning to think from my heart space I began to think bigger thoughts and imagine more than I ever thought possible before working with him. I did more energy work. I started meditating and doing yoga daily. I started to feel like a different person. A happier person. A healthier person. A calmer person. I liked who I was becoming and the route I was taking.

It was now just about two weeks away from my trip to Las Vegas. I was excited and nervous. I remembered John telling me in Costa Rica that I should cut my cords energetically with my ex-boyfriend. I still thought of him often. I decided it was a good time to cut the cords before meeting with Spiritual Man again. I booked a session with John and he cut the cords. It was refreshing – I felt myself detach from my ex and a huge heaviness lifted from me. I wish I had done this sooner. Why didn't I do this in Costa Rica? At the end of the session, John had a vision of a gift that appeared for me from the Universe. It was an ankh. The ankh in ancient Egypt is known as the key of life. It was the ancient Egyptian hieroglyphic character that read "eternal life". The ankh represented a new direction, a new beautiful and lively beginning.

COACHING TIP: Move towards everything that brings your soul pure child-like joy. That is your path.

I Attract What I Am · *Melissa Dawn*

Chapter 10

The Ankh Awakening

I was preparing to leave for Las Vegas for the HR Technology event. The company I worked for was testing the market for an innovative HR product on employee engagement and I truly believed in this product because I felt I was contributing to making employees happier at work. There was a lot to prepare and I was really excited about the event, both professionally and personally – professionally because I had put so much time in marketing a product and the event and personally because I would get to see Spiritual Man again.

I went to book the hotel and I noticed that the Luxor Hotel and Casino had a special. Seeing that an ankh came out in my journeying with John Germain Leto, The Lux seemed like the right place as it was full of Egyptian hieroglyphics so Spiritual Man and I agreed to meet there. I stepped out into the Vegas air and it felt warm and exciting. I couldn't believe how lucky I was to have such beautiful opportunities in my life, including a company that trusted me enough to take charge of their marketing. I got into a taxi and headed for the Lux. It had been four months since we last saw each other. What will it be like to see him again? Would we feel the same way? I thought the worst-case scenario would be that we could still hang out as friends if there was no more chemistry between us.

I arrived at the hotel. Spiritual Man greeted me at the entrance. He hugged me. It felt so natural – like I was in the right place. And with the hieroglyphics and ankhs engraved in the decor of the hotel, I felt that the Universe was confirming this. Everything was flowing beautifully. We went to the casino and he showed me how to play blackjack. It was fun. I really got into it and we even made some money. I felt good with him.

We spent the weekend together having meaningful conversations about hopes and dreams, enjoying Vegas together. He was ambitiously working on writing a movie that he also wanted to produce. Our time together was beautiful. I didn't want the weekend to end. Sunday night Spiritual Man headed back to LA after agreeing that we will keep in touch and let the Universe take it from there.

I had to rest and get myself ready for the trade show. It was hard to switch mindset from cloud romance to corporate, but I had to. The company was paying for me to be there and I had to deliver. The trade show went really well. I did some amazing presentations. I got some really big companies to sign up as beta users of the product. My boss was truly impressed. I also loved the fact I could apply a lot of what I was learning in my coaching to the product itself and to the people at the trade show. Talking to Senior HR people and VP's I realized that I was able to better connect with them because of my coaching training. I felt everything I was doing was leading to something much, much bigger.

Just two years earlier I was at my worst. Two divorces, failed love life, single mom, emotional pain holding in my body and my heart, feeling like everything was a dead end and now I realize that we can be the captains of our ship. The more we work on ourselves, the more we remove patterns that don't serve us, the more open we become to all the magic and miracles out there waiting for us to grab. I was on to something big here. This was good. My coaching, energy work and therapy were pulling all aspects of me and my big life ideas together and yielding great results.

COACHING TIP: When we go with the flow of life instead of our fixed vision, we open up to something bigger than we could have ever imagined.

Chapter 11

Fulfillment

Back from Vegas, I had to keep moving forward. I was excited about my coaching path. The next three-day coaching weekend arrived, this one was about Fulfillment. Little did I know this weekend would hugely impact my life, moving forward. I was so happy to be back in the room with likeminded people on a similar path as my own. I felt so close to them. Amongst many other things, that weekend, we learned how to determine our core values, create our life purpose statement and connect to our highest selves. These tools were life changing. Once you know your core values and your life purpose, you can make all your decisions based around them. When your choices are aligned with your core values and life purpose, you know you're on the right path. If not, then it means you need to re-route. If you're unsure of your core values, please use this exercise to determine what they are. www. CEOofYour.Life/values/

I identified my core values as: real, brave, fun, freedom, integrity, passion, health, spirituality and success. And I declared my life purpose as: "I am the energizing bunny that guides you in creating an orgasmically joyful life and business." I must admit the whole class got a good laugh from it. And from then on, I was known as "orgasmically joyful." If you look up orgasmic in the dictionary it says "very enjoyable or exciting." To me, orgasmically joyful means being extremely happy and loving life. This was my purpose. From that day forward, I awoke every morning saying my life purpose statement out loud and allowing it to sink in so I'd show up in the world with this joyful excited energy. It was working!

These tools gave me a better understanding of who I am. I felt much better in my skin. I felt like I was finally getting to know the real me. Not the 'me' that family, friends, teachers, bosses and others had programmed me to believe I should be but who I truly was. This gave me so much confidence. I felt connected to my true self. I had never felt this connection before. It was beautiful. On top of being clear on my purpose and values, I now knew how to connect with my highest self: the part of you that wants the best for you. The part of you that is clear and knowing – the part of you that loves you unconditionally. I felt really powerful with these tools. I felt like I was telling the world to watch out, the real Melissa Dawn has arrived.

How could I use these tools in my branding? John Germain Leto was right. My original website was not a true reflection of me. It was based on what I thought was good based on what others were doing and based on my business schooling and experience. I needed to create a website and brand that reflected my core values and my purpose. After all, when people look for a coach, the only thing to make me stand out from other coaches is my true self. As Meryl Streep says: "What makes you different or weird – that is your strength."

So my branding and marketing based on the real me had begun. Looking at my core values – which three did I want to choose to reflect as my brand? I chose real, brave and fun. This needed to be explicitly reflected in my content, in my pictures; these values were my essence they had to shine through in all my communications. Not just in my business, but me as a person as well. I contacted Tee Tran, a high school friend who had become a photographer and told him my intentions, my values and what I want to create. He said: "No worries Melissa, we will do a photo shoot that will reflect that." And we did. John helped me decide what to wear for my photo shoot and Tee Tran and his wife, Bao Han, chose backgrounds and poses that made my true self and values shine. These images show that I am down to earth, fun and brave. Tee Tran captured every moment. I was so grateful to have amazing creative people contribute to building my brand.

I decided to use my life purpose statement as my tagline: "Create an orgasmically joyful life & business." Now this was a brave statement. I ran the tagline by some friends and was told it was too risky. It was too out there. They told me people would think I was a sex coach. Then I ran it by some of my clients and was told that if they had seen that tagline before hiring me, they probably would have thought twice. Only two of my fellow coaching colleagues and my own coach supported my tagline. Out of about 50 people polled, all advised me against it. I had been a business and marketing professional for the past 20 years. Would this diminish my credibility in other people's eyes? Would they find me crazy or unprofessional? Also... what would my Dad think? Almost everyone polled was ardently against the tagline and all the while, my gut was saying "This is right for you Melissa. It's brave, just like you. It's honest, just like you. It's playful and fun... just like you!

It was really a struggle for me. In my core, I believed

the tagline was a true representation of who I am and the message I wanted to convey. After all, who truly doesn't want to have an orgasmically joyful life and business?

I realized that it is one thing is to know your values and another thing entirely to put those values out there in the professional sphere – to actually be a living expression of your values in all aspects of your life. After all, if I feel I need to hide who I really am, how can I coach others to live their lives being true to who they are?

So "Create an Orgasmically Joyful Life & Business" would be the official tagline. And as my coach said, if it didn't work out, we could always change it. I worked hard on creating the website. I had to ask some hard questions. What type of coach did I want to be? What type of clients did I want to work with? What type of clients fueled me? Notice I was not asking what the market was looking for. I was starting my marketing with an inside analysis.

Question 1: What type of work brings out the best in me?

For me, the answer was simple; working with people that want to feel passionate about their life and create a life that is a true reflection of them, not what others want for them. Guiding clients on how to be the CEO of their life, how to discover their gifts and bring them forward into both their personal and professional life. It's something I know intimately and have worked hard on myself to learn to do. I'm living that dream and I know how to help people do the same for themselves.

ANALYSIS

OF

THE WORRY TRICK

How Your Brain Tricks You into Expecting the Worst and What You Ca Do About It

A FastReads Book Analysis with Key Takeaways & Review

TABLE OF CONTENTS

SYNOPSIS

e Worry Trick: How Your Brain Tricks You into Expecting the Worst 'hat You Can Do About It, renowned psychologist, anxiety coach and ‍: of the bestselling book *The Panic Attacks Workbook,* Dr. David ‍nell exposes the human body's natural trick responsible for chronic ‍ and proceeds to prescribe an antidote to restore control over worry ‍gain your life.

‍nell starts by reviewing the body's natural setting in handling worry, ‍bserves that the human mindset on worry preparedness is dominated ‍: amygdala—an organ that interrupts the brain's reasonable synthesis ‍iger and activates the 'fight or flight' mode, blurring the human ability ‍ceive danger accurately. The book deeply discusses the way worry ‍rs fire reflexively, and therefore why to defeat worry, a person must ‍e the reflexive worry trick through a dedicated cognitive restructuring ‍am.

‍ribing to the already popular Cognitive Behavioral Therapy and ‍limenting this with an emerging cognitive recalibration method, ‍tance and Commitment Therapy (ACT), the author sets out on a ‍ey to teach the body to accept the worry trigger as its own and work ‍ds resolving the unnecessary results of this worry through some ‍gent 'counter-tricks.'

‍ig these include the use of songs to depict worry in a way that is lighter ‍: brain, use of a secondary language to talk about the worry, use of pig ‍ or an equivalent corruption of language to talk about the worry, use ‍ericks or Haikus, and general therapy.

‍y, the author explores the benefits of using humor to tone down the ‍ʌ, as well as the benefits of adequate and regular sleep in combating ‍ffects associated with worry.

BOOK REVIEW

David Carbonell follows up his earlier work, *Panic Attacks Workboo* this sequel *The Worry Trick* and brings out his more than two deca experience in anxiety treatment as a clinical psychologist.

In his book, the author takes on the impossible task of subduing the condition, especially excessive or chronic worry, using cog restructuring or de-fusion methods. In the book title, the thematic h suggests helping the reader understand the way the brain profile worrying scenario, starting on a purely physiological level and advanc a behavioral or operational one. Next, the author promises to presc method or program for defeating the body's natural wiring in a manne reduces the effect of worry without compromising the effective purpo which this natural setting was designed.

In handling the body's physiology, the book looks at the parts of the albeit superficially in its first two chapters, and explores the two crucial parts in worry management: the amygdala and the cerebral c The author goes into as much detail as the nature of the book allo explaining that the cerebral cortex is the primary part of the responsible for the evaluation of sensory information from the exteric interior sensors such as eyes, ears, and hormone synthesis and cc centers. The cerebral cortex is a procedural organ that takes its tir carefully evaluate a potential threat and rate it accurately, usually avo the worry threshold altogether.

Next, the author looks at the amygdala and describes it as a short circ the main danger analysis center—the cerebral cortex. The amy bypasses the cerebral cortex in danger synthesis, instantly activatin 'fight, flight or freeze mode', a regular companion of the worrying state author then clearly depicts the amygdala as a vital organ which, despi obviously misleading role in worry trigger, rapidly helps people e dangerous situations within response times the cerebral cortex typi cannot achieve.

In the first chapter, the author's explanation of the physiological and effective in a book aimed for the layman worrier, and adequately ...es the reader for the following sections. This style is in tandem with ...sed in *Panic Attacks Workbook* in which the reader similarly adapts ...y way of biologically describing the circumstances of panic attacks. ...s a necessary style, given that the book's thematic presentation is ...l towards the general reader. A notable point on the author's ...itation of his work is the use of short sections separated by headlined ...aries or theme titles. This trend not only eliminates the possible ...tony and thought sublimation that can occasion lengthy monologues, ...lps the reader feel in control of the content they read.

...nell spends ample time presenting the quality of worry and how it is ...ered and recalled from the active and the subconscious parts of the ... He explains why the brain re-lives the memory of a past danger ...ience every time a 'worry cue' arises in the environment, such as a ..., sight, smell or person that was a key aspect in the original worry or ...r scenario. The book occasionally uses examples from the author's ...e practice in order to supplement an argument. This helps in ...lidating a strong case in defense of his views, and aids the reader in ...ng with the external worry environment to stop feeling alone and ...gated.

...laining the Acceptance and Commitment Therapy, the author uses the ...gy of thought fusion, where the brain replaces the scenario of a past ...ive experience in another, totally different environment, and proceeds ...ct to this new perception with the evaluation of danger from the past .. The book uses precise examples of the suitcase transferred between ... which still retains its contents, and the girl who, after experiencing a ...tack, irrationally associates the word cat with the total experience of ...ctual attack. The book clearly presents this sequence of logic and ...ssfully implants in the reader's mind a solid cause-effect relationship ...een perception of danger and chronic worry. This section ends with the ...nent for a brain-changing alternative to the worrying pattern, which is ...ssence of cognitive restructuring and cognitive behavioral therapy. This ...on, arguably one of the most technical, is devoid of the anticipated ...n that almost unavoidably forms mind behavior discussions. It meets

the intended objective while steering clear of the confusing and
complex language.

In the following chapters, Carbonell maps out the therapies themselves
the ACT and CBT. These concepts are assumed to be new to most re
The book suggests the use of methods that encourage the mind
experience the worry triggers so constantly that their danger
diminishes due to familiarity. In depth, the author advises against th
avoidance or suppression, stating the effects of not fully facing the v
Again, the book revisits the worry duality scenario where people who
may do it either because they believe in the validity of an invalid
trigger, or do not hold the original worry thought as a valid reason in
In the case of the latter, one therefore worries that they worry too
about unnecessary conditions, causing additional and unwarranted wo
a self-fulfilling and vicious cycle. While the use of these concepts is h
for the reader, the author tends to repeat similar cases throughout the
This repetition is justified, however, in that accounts of his experience
clients must have shared reasoning in order to more fully suppo
argument. The repetition is additionally mitigated by the uniqueness
cases the author describes.

In the final section detailing ACT therapy, the chapters tend to be a
brief, especially considering the purpose of the book is to provide me
of overcoming worry. The book mentions and briefly explains the u
songs, limericks and haiku, which can be used to dilute the subcons
worry through focus on the rhyming lines or poetic nature of th
Expression of the worry in a language other than the usual spoken o
language, or use of bastardized languages such as pig Latin can sim
help to change the way the brain perceives and processes worry.

The author could have more deeply explained the workings of
methods at the subconscious level to inspire in the reader a stronger l
in their efficacy. In addition, use of more real-life experiences with pa
utilizing these therapies may have given the aspiring reader
confidence, or more realism, and better informed them of the exp
results after adopting this therapy.

ll, the book is accessible, easy to read, and informative, and a strong on to the genre of anxiety and stress management. As the author states opening section, this book will be useful to those who worry too those who care for those who worry too much, those who worry that worry too much, and everyone in between.

KEY THEMES

The Worry Trick

If only worry were predictable, everybody would have a way of avoid
In the first chapter, the writer starts by giving an example of how h
developed jaundice (a common condition among newborns) whi
treatable. But due to the anxiety and worry that had consumed him a
wife, even after confirmation from the doctor that their son would be
they still were not satisfied.

The author introduces the worry trick—a way through which your
sneaks worry into your active thought flow without your volu
involvement. In the first chapter, the author asserts that worrying
dangerous, it's just discomfort that one feels when faced with uncerta

*"When you get tricked into treating the discomfort of doubt as if it
dangerous, this leads you to struggle against the doubt, trying to remo*
unwanted thoughts from mind" (Carbonell, Ch. 1).

Through the example of two characters—Scott and Ann, the book s
the negative side of worry. Ann has a social anxiety disorder that make
hate social places for fear of being judged, while Scott spends much
time worrying about his job, as a result of which he worries that he w
too much. Ann and Scott represent a lot of people who go through wo
disproportionate extents.

In the ensuing worry chain, worries tend to increase rather than disap
a trend that leads to chronic worry, and potentially to adverse effects.

The Nature of Worry

In chapter four, the author explains how people experience worry. The
manifestation is physical and includes heart racing, upset ston
sweating, trembling, labored breathing and other sensations. The seco
behavioral and includes nail biting, hair pulling, and other comm

iors. The third method is all in the mind and results in becoming
us.

chapter, the book demonstrates how people struggle with worry in
that maintain rather than remove it, and shows how much easier
g with worry would be if only one could cultivate an accepting
le towards the thoughts of chronic worry.

ying is part of the human condition, but when some people struggle
hronic worry they often think they are unusual. The book points out
eople get fooled by comparing other people's outer appearances to
hey feel inside. In chapter two, the author talks about how we relate to
ing and how they got to the point of being chronic worriers.

uthor additionally looks at the diverse nature of worry. Some people
experience occasional worry about ordinary problems and treat this as
casional nuisance they can dismiss. If this works for them, it is a good
as they don't have to worry much about their worries. However, others
ind themselves in constant worry, a condition which can potentially
te into a worry duality status.

most important aspect of this chronic relationship with worry,
ver, is not the amount of worry but the way to respond to it" (David
nell, Ch. 2).

ook explains, from the author's experience with his clients, how worry
ns become frustrated by the chain of thoughts which increase in a
nce of catastrophes; they are present in their usual environment but
lly focusing on future disasters, the likelihood of which is low.

uthor believes that there exists a successful way to handle worry, that
anging one's relationship with worry rather than trying to change the
. You can do this by writing worries down so you can do a little work
em, put them in a lineup and cross-examine them. However, the
ss is not as easy as it sounds. People who are stuck in chronic worry
diting their thoughts into more realistic versions somehow less helpful
hey hope. Ultimately, what you worry about is not nearly as important

The Worry Duality

Worry has a duality relationship with its victims: you are eith
acceptance of the circumstances that inspire your worry and the
looking to resolve the worry, or you do not view the circumstances as a
cause for worry—and therefore are worried that you worry too much
things you shouldn't worry about. This rotary confusion of thoughts f
fire that ultimately leads you to chronic worry.

To illustrate this, the author talks about a case he handled when h
training to become a psychologist, his first experience working with a
who struggled with worry. According to him, the patient tended to ove
the good things he did at work and overemphasized the things that n
improvement. For therapy, the author asked the client to defocu
negatives and focus on the positives. He was surprised when his client
back only looking more worried about not worrying.

Carbonell maps out two possible paths consistent with people who
handling worry: some people try to protect their thoughts against da
while others try to prove that there isn't any danger, so they can feel
and stop worrying. They look for ways to disprove the threats and rea
themselves that the feared catastrophes won't come to pass. Regardl
the strategies they apply to subdue worry, in either case, worry victim

Clearly, the author's direction through the third and fourth chapters is
working approach would have to face worry head-on, rather than atter
shut it out or dodge it.

Looking for Worry

The fourth and fifth chapters target those who are bothered by a
worries. If you keep worrying that your worries mean there is some
wrong with you, then you will keep getting tricked into responding in
that make your worries worse.

The author notes that this is a condition that was not so common in the
Today, people spend more time "in their heads," processing inform

st, our ancestors focused on dealing with the physical objects in their
nment—they handled instantaneous threats and lived in the moment.

example, the book documents how people who expect to get worried
sappointed when no worry is forthcoming, essentially worrying that
re not worried. An example that serves as comic relief is the author's
on how people today buy horror movies, knowing full well the
ted reactions after watching them. People want to feel scared, they
o feel horrified and worried—even subconsciously.

e who have experienced worry constantly tend to look forward to it,
f it kills them. Handling worry, therefore, must be a bold and strong
at restructures the very nature of the victim's cognitive alignment.

y and Counter-intuition

pter five, the author explains how wrongly people deal with worry.
hapter instructs how to apply the rule of opposites—asserting that
is a counterintuitive problem that needs a counterintuitive response,
servation that tells you your gut feeling on how to handle worry is
y wrong.

ht of this, it is no wonder that the harder you try to solve the problem
onic worry, the worse it gets. The chapter explains in depth how this
ns. Psychological research on the subject of thought suppression
y shows that,

*e main effect of thought suppression is a resurgence of the thoughts
e trying to forget"* (David Carbonell, Ch. 5).

the author illustrates some experiments to try and control human
hts, which proves impossible, an indication that we can only control
we feel and not what we think.

ndling anxiety, the first rule of thumb governs your interactions with
xternal world around you—the harder you try and the more you
gle, the more you are likely to get what you want by making every

The other is the one pertaining to your internal world of thoughts, em
and physical sensation—this is different in the sense that the mo
oppose your thoughts and emotions the more of them you will have.

The third rule, the rule of opposites, applies to a lot of anxiety sympt
well as to chronic worry. The worry trick is a powerful influence, a
writer helps us understand what gives it so much power in this chapt

The WHAT IT and WHY of Worry

You can learn how to accept the worrisome thoughts and deal wi
worry. In chapter six, the author introduces the two words that are
vocabulary of a worrier: WHAT IF, and WHY. These words are
signals in dealing with worry, but usually are not noticeable by c
worriers.

"What if" introduces the worry. Most people generally don't think abc
good stuff when it comes to these two words, it's all negative and dr
things that could happen in the future.

The author tells you how you can easily become more aware of the W
trigger. He helps the readers by giving them an exercise on how to
their worries. One of the examples is buying *Tic Tac* chewing gur
every time you notice the feeling "what if," you eat a piece or toss it
garbage. This will help you keep count of the number of times
experience a "what if."

With this exercise, the writer helps his readers become increasingly a
of the habit and how to deal with it. Worrying leads to people feeling w
and more pessimistic about their future, but you shouldn't take
seriously. The book encourages the readers in disregarding the "bait
so often lures people into making their worry more persistent.

tance and Commitment Therapy (ACT), and the
itive Behavioral Therapy (CBT)

two therapies are the author's primary tools of handling and vely managing worry.

efforts to directly reduce anxiety will increase it" (David Carbonell,

tance and commitment therapy (rule of the opposite) emphasizes the veness of dealing with your thoughts, drawn from the concept of ive fusion, in managing worry. It has two parts: acceptance and itment. You must accept your worry circumstances, not circumvent lge them, as the first step towards resolution. Secondly, there is d a commitment part—you closely follow a pre-set therapy routine structures your cognitive structure and allows you to see the worry its differently than when they were imprinted into your thought ses.

CT uses the example of a girl who is so afraid of cats after an unate encounter in which she is attacked and scratched by a cat that n't stand to hear or even think of the word cat. So severe is her worry ats that people around her use other words to describe a cat to avoid g her.

uthor defines and explains the concepts of cognitive fusion—wrongly iating words with the actions they depict—and de-fusion, which s the effects of cognitive fusion.

itive Behavioral Therapy (CBT) applies in its original sense in ating worry. The mechanism and effectiveness of using CBT ined with the ACT, are explained in depth in chapters eight and nine, n extension throughout the rest of the book.

ks to Defeat Worry

uthor devotes a significant section of the book to share ideas on how

defeating intrusion of worry thoughts. For instance, you can sing a c
song with themes on worry that helps you deal with hearing the v
words—this is a form of the ACT. Secondly, you may write a limeri
short five-line poem with interesting rhyme patterns, to help your cogr
structure de-link your mind from the worry.

In addition, you may conceive your worry thoughts and go over then
second language if you are bilingual, or use pig Latin or a similar corru
of English or your original language that allows you to thin
communicate your thoughts without actually mentioning the words
trigger your worry.

The author however advises against trying to forget the worry though
this will render the entire therapy inconsequential. Instead, he advises I
active as opposed to being busy. In other words, keep at the therapy
handle your worries constantly in the proper manner (by song or lim
or another language). The thoughts will go away in their own way and

Worry Workout

As an actual part of worry therapy, the author lays out methods one ca
to change the worrying trend in the long term. The first method is ado
meditation as a daily routine and part of your lifestyle. The specific ber
of meditation are many and far-reaching, generally improving your ov
health and boosting your wellbeing—results that reduce effects of wor

The second activity is setting up 'appointments' with worry. This n
you devote your full attention to worrying and nothing else. In this cha
the writer explains that worry should be faced head-on rather
postponed or wished away. The author suggests a routine of pass
observing your thoughts as they come and go while you focus on somet
basic like your breathing.

Regaining Life After Worry

In the last chapters of his book, the author explores the parasitic natu

your entire life. The book suggests ways of regaining your life after
ating your worry trends. In addition, the book looks at the importance
ficient and regular sleep in restoring your health.

ter 13 recognizes the difficulty of regular sleep for people who have
red chronic worry, and suggests effective ways of luring sleep back
heir lives.

p is an activity that doesn't respond well to effort" (David Carbonell,
3).

ext chapter expounds on the importance of humoring your worry. The
r asserts that worry is hard to deal with, and is best managed with a
humor.

*ponding to chronic worry without humor is like drilling a tooth without
anesthesia"* (David Carbonell, Ch. 14).

you have reached this point, you may go back to living your life. On
terms.

KEY TAKEAWAYS

Key Takeaway: Your thoughts are important—they are reason you are alive.

If you have ever had to deal with worry, especially if you are aware tha worry and that it is affecting the quality of your life, you may wisl didn't have thoughts at all. You are wrong! Your thoughts keep you out of danger, allow you to fit in a social setting and help you in many ways. In other words, your thoughts are you. You should always take of your thoughts, you are responsible for them and how you deal with determines how you deal with the outside world.

Key Takeaway: It's okay to worry, everybody does it. Bu worry smart.

Because there's no off-switch to your brain's worry triggers and no si way to stop worrisome thoughts, you should not feel abnormal about w Don't try to stop your thoughts, this will only make your worry w Instead, learn and practice simple but effective mechanisms through v you can manage your worry. On the same thought, don't place too importance to not worrying, it is an indicator of a stable state of mi which you are in control of your present circumstances—the circumstances you can face and control anyway. You shouldn't go loc for worry; nurture your internal environment to allow worry and to reg it when it comes—you will be fine.

Key Takeaway: Doubt is no danger, just discomfort.

It's natural to be doubtful. When you have the right attitude towards d you will triumph—just avoid overthinking. Trying to go about your business is an amazing exercise that doesn't involve much but effect makes the worry fade away. Be patient with yourself while managing w

Takeaway: The Worry Trick is actually nature's doing.

brain is made to recognize and fight danger quicker than the danger to get to you. Your amygdala is a short circuit in your 'fight or flight' n that accelerates your impulses and shortens your response time, ly helping you avoid danger. Unfortunately, the amygdala is tive—it does not consult widely and wisely before rating danger and ng worry. Managing worry, therefore, has everything to do with ing your response system to slow down and re-think the danger cues e pushing the buttons.

do not need to fight your amygdala for deceiving you into worry every it may have impulsively saved you from being hit by an oncoming at the flicker of a moment. Just teach your mind to erase worry data your subconscious when the time is right.

Take away: Acceptance and Commitment Therapy and nitive Behavioral Therapy are the best tools to defeat ry.

deals with restructuring the way you perceive danger and your worry ns, relying on the power of helping you face your fears in a controlled g. CBT also helps your mind recognize, accept and prepare to handle erceived danger, but in a more direct and aggressive setting. The ty of these therapies is that they will successfully help you manage worry condition.

can use limericks, songs, Haikus or pig Latin languages to defeat the y blueprint. It is easy and enjoyable to do this.

Takeaway: Sleep well, meditate, and use humor when ing about your worries.

t give worries all your time. Learn to allow sleep to come, and when it sleep sufficiently and regularly. Let meditation appeal to your internal

humor is a very effective way of managing your worries. Humor make
moments lighter, and supplements the principals of the ACT in defe
the worry trick in that it undermines your body's perception of danger

BACKGROUND ON AUTHOR

avid Carbonell, Ph.D., is a Chicago based clinical psychologist and
thor of two bestselling books *Panic Attacks Workbook*, and *The Worry
*. Dr. Carbonell specializes in the treatment of disorders including
, social anxiety, generalized anxiety, and obsessive-compulsive
der, as well as common and chronic phobias.

is more than 25 years of experience in his field of expertise and is the
r of Anxiety Treatment Center Ltd, Greater Chicago. He is licensed by
linois and New York and is a member of the American Psychological
ciation, the Association for Behavioral and Cognitive Therapies, the
ciation for Contextual and Behavioral Science, the Anxiety Disorders
ciation of America, and the International Association for Cognitive
otherapy. Currently, he is also the mentor in the anxiety coaching
te www.anxietycoach.com.

Carbonell attended DePaul University (1985), and earlier Syracuse
ersity (1972) from which he graduated with a degree in political
ce.

COMMENDED READING:

Anxiety Solution: A Quieter Mind, a Calmer You
hloe Brotheridge

e Anxiety Solution: A Quieter Mind, a Calmer You, Chloe Brotheridge
ops and applies a program of managing and combating the effects of
nd stress in women, both young and aged.

r book, Brotheridge helps you identify signs of stress and anxiety
e it gets out of control, and prescribes easy and effective ways of
ty management including daily exercise and meditation, as well as a
rehensive alarm response arrangement. If you are a woman who needs
fe back from the crippling effects of anxiety and panic, this book is for

Why We Are Wired To Worry and How Neuroscience Will Help Fix It: Stop Stressing, Reduce Anxiety, Feel Happy, Finally! **by Sharie Spironhi**

In this 225-page workbook of distilled research and development, S Spironhi will help you re-engineer your life and take charge of w anxiety and low mood by teaching you how your brain works.

The book will tell you the chemical balance that your brain's amy commands to combat and manage worry and anxiety using three chemicals: dopamine, oxytocin, and serotonin. You will learn a simple routine you can use to trigger the proper brain environment to help yc in the indestructible mood and effectively live your life on your own t

OTHER TITLES BY DR. DAVID CARBONELL:

Panic Attacks Workbook: A Guided Program for Beating the Panic Trick (2004)

END

you enjoyed this analysis, please leave an honest review on Amazon.com. It'd mean a lot to us.

ou haven't already, we encourage you to purchase a copy of the original book.

Here are some other titles from FastReads we think you may enjoy:

Summary of The Subtle Art of Not Giving a F*ck by Mark Manson

Summary of Feeling Good by David D. Burns

Summary of The Obstacle Is the Way by Ryan Holiday

Question 2: What type of clients fuel me?

The people who we work with have a huge influence on the enjoyment of our work. Loving your clients is just as important as loving the work you do with them. To me, the type of clients that fuel me are people who truly want to move forward – clients who are into personal growth. Clients who want to create heart-based lives and businesses, businesses they love to work at all day long even if they don't get paid (even though they also want to make good money, of course). I believe everything is interconnected: If something isn't working in your personal life, it will affect your business (and vice versa). I truly believe in taking a holistic approach and I work best with clients who are on the same page. So there it was. I did some deep internal analysis and had my answers and my content. I was ready to officially launch my website.

COACHING TIP: In everything you do, always start with an internal analysis; always start with you. Ask yourself what you truly want and what you want to create based on what fuels you, your values and your life purpose.

Chapter 12

The Launch

There were advantages to being single – I could put all my focus and energy during my free time into building my website and marketing. It took about three months to build everything and to create my first eBook. I was so proud; my website was a true reflection of me. You could go on my site and literally feel my energy and personality. Before launching, I set my intention with my Shaman for it to attract the people I was meant to serve. We asked for a Divine blessing on it. After doing so, I was sure the Universe had my back on the new direction I was undertaking. I launched my website and shared the launch on Facebook. I got so much love and support coming my way, that I felt just like a kid receiving everything she ever wanted. The orgasmically joyful tagline was a hit. People loved it. It got them intrigued. I did not get a single sleazy comment about it. That weekend I went to another one of my three-day coaching training weekends and my colleagues praised my website. Two of them even approached me asking if I could give them business coaching to help them create their brand. Wow. Two new clients just like that – and exactly the kind of clients I wanted to work with. How could it get even better than this?

I was sooooo happy! With all the excitement of launching my coaching website and another coaching training weekend, I had to drag my feet back to my marketing job the next Monday. I was less and less into it. All I wanted to do was coach all day long. I still gave 100 percent of myself to my job but my heart wasn't in it. I applied my coaching skills to my marketing job just to keep me going at it, but it soon felt more like a chore than a job because all I wanted to do was coach full time.

I then put out to the Universe, asking how I could spend more time doing what I love. Be careful what you ask the Universe because two weeks later the Universe came back with a response – one I was totally not expecting.

My boss called me into the office and told me some important funding the company had been expecting would be delayed for a few months. He said he could only pay half of my salary until the funding came in. What a shock! I was scared. I had not expected this and asked myself how would I be able to quickly make up the difference in income? I was a single mom. After about 24 hours, the shock wore off and I realized this was a GIFT. The Universe gifted me with this so I could spend more time building my coaching business. So now, how was I to get more clients? I decided to hit LinkedIn. Yes, I hit LinkedIn with my orgasmically joyful headline. I knew this was a risk on something as corporate as LinkedIn, but this was who I was and this is what I was putting out there. I made my summary and skills more "sexy" to read and I sent personal messages to all my connections announcing my new business, website and my first free eBook 10 Steps Towards An Orgasmically Joyful Life & Career (you can get it here: http://melissadawn.ca/ebook. php) please note my second free eBook is 9 Steps Towards An Orgasmically Joyful Life & Business which you can get here: www.CEOofYour.Life/ebook/ and my latest one, 6 Steps To Determine Your Core Values guide so you can become a living expression of them! You can get it here: www.CEOofYour.Life/values/

My personal messages worked out. I got some new clients and I made up the difference in my salary that month. I also decided to incorporate my company. I called it CEO of Your Life. My mission was to guide as many people as possible to become the CEO of their lives – meaning to go for what they truly want and live life their way. Their life, their way. I was so proud to officially have my own company.

Although I was happy with the way my coaching business was taking off, I felt like I was missing a partner in my personal life. I wanted to start looking into finding my soulmate for real this time. The man I envisioned just a few months ago. I knew he was there and I knew I would meet him that year. I decided to write out exactly what I wanted this man to be like. I wrote about seven pages with all the details I could think of, including his looks, his personality, what we would do together, how he would be with my son, how amazing our love-making would be, and how much we would laugh and enjoy each other in every way. I was determined to attract this man. How was I going to do it?

It's my belief that to get different results one must do something differently. I started following a whole bunch of dating coaches. I signed up to their newsletters, watched their videos and followed them on social media.

After a month, I chose one to sign up with. I had an

OK feeling about him and their offer but after I paid I found out that I would not be working with the coach I had been in touch with, rather, one that he had trained. To work with the original coach would have cost even more money.

I had sent this coach information about me being a single mom, my business and other details and he didn't even take the time to read about me before our session. We had our first coaching call and it was horrible. I was being trained at the Coaches Training Institute to ask powerful questions so the person you are coaching opens their mind, connects within and finds the answers that are good for them. This coach told me what to do. He didn't ask me any questions. He coached me to do things that didn't fit into my circumstances and at one point I asked him, "How can I date every night when I am a single mom and have my son most of the time?" to which he replied: "I didn't know you were a single mom." He didn't read my emails nor did he take the time to ask questions – he worked from a cookie cutter format that he used for everyone. I was turned off and I was angry. He wasn't competent. I contacted the head coach, asked for a refund to which he replied that he'd coach me but I'd get fewer sessions because he's more expensive. No refunds. They had me trapped. I agreed to his conditions, we had one session together, it was fine but again, not a single powerful question was asked of me, just more of "here's what to do."

That's when I realized the importance of hiring a certified coach. Yes, there are plenty of coaches out there that make a lot of money – but not all are certified. The quality you get with a certified coach is not comparable. You need to find your own answers. Only you know the path that is right for you and you need a professional to help you find that path, not dictate that path.

I tried to keep an open mind to his style of coaching but soon realized that he was just a good talker. He himself wasn't even in a long-term relationship. Why did I hire a coach who was not where I wanted to be? I should have hired a coach that was in an orgasmically committed joyful relationship. The coaching sessions were going nowhere. I was not impressed. I didn't pay all this money just to hear this. I tried to get out of these coaching sessions, but he refused to give me a refund. I tried to get money back via PayPal but it had been more than 30 days since I paid so I was no longer entitled to ask for one. What did I learn from this? Always choose a coach who is where you want to be. I needed a coach who was spiritual and not just telling me what to do but who would help me with the energy work I needed in order to attract the right person.

COACHING TIPS:

1) To get different results, you need to do something different.

2) There are good coaches and there are not-so-good coaches. Everyone resonates with different people. You can learn from even a bad coach. You can learn what you don't want so moving forward; you are more aware of what you do want.

3) When looking for a coach, look for one who is where

you want to be and that is aligned with your values.

4) Whenever you are in a situation you are not happy with, ask yourself: "What did I learn from this?"

Chapter 13

Calling HIM In....

I went back to my Shaman, John Germain Leto, and told him about my experience with the nightmare dating coach. He said, "Why didn't you come to see me?" I can help you do the energy work you need to attract your soul mate. Dating to-do lists don't work." Duh! Why didn't I go straight to John? I guess I still didn't realize the power of energy work. John asked me, "Would you like to call in your soul mate?" Oh my, I didn't even know that was possible. He said when you work with the Universe, the highest source, you call in the highest soul mate for you. "Of course, this is what I truly want," I replied. We did an energy session in which I met with my soul mate in the Universe. He was amazing. He was so loving. It was magical. It felt like paradise; I wanted to stay there forever. John said: "The next one you meet will be the one. I see the engagement ring. It's already done."

I left our session feeling so excited! He was on his way. I immediately made room for him in my home. I emptied out drawers in the bedroom and bathroom to make room for his stuff. I was ready for him. I was creating space for him in every way in my life. I began to wonder: When would he show up? How would he show up? What would it be like? I started to become impatient and kept asking the Universe, when? But you know the Universe works on its own time. I had to learn how to trust Divine Timing.

I went to visit my Toastmaster's club and bumped

into John Chu, one of my Toastmaster colleagues who is a hypnotist. I told him about all the work I did, about how my soul mate was on his way and that I wanted to expedite his arrival however I could. He told me: "Give me four sessions with you and he'll show up. Whatever energy you're giving off is not bringing him in. We'll remove it." He said this with such confidence that I said yes to the four sessions. After just two sessions with him, I felt as if a huge weight had been lifted off my shoulders. We addressed some traumas that seemed to hinder me; I was not putting out the right energy to attract the right person for me. Now I was feeling as light as a feather. I could not believe those incidents had weighed so heavily on me. I was carrying them around without even noticing. I could see the benefits of John Chu's work and I was grateful. I continued to work with him for a few months.

COACHING TIP: Trust in Divine timing. Things will happen when they are meant to happen. The Universe has your back. Trust. And, don't worry about how.

I Attract What I Am • *Melissa Dawn*

Chapter 14

July 23rd

July 23rd was a date that represented new beginnings for me. It was on a July 23rd quite a few years earlier that my first ex-husband and I had our first separation. This July 23rd, I had the premonition of a new beginning. The company I was working for was having a barbecue after work, along with the other companies in the building. For some reason, I was more excited about it than I would normally be for a regular barbecue. After work we went up to the terrace of our building. My colleagues were cooking up Brazilian sausages and making Caipirinhas, Brazil's national cocktail. I had done some marketing consulting for one of the other companies in the building and I loved the fact that we intermingled professionally. Even though we were separate companies, we all were willing to help each other out with whatever was needed.

I was speaking to Marcos, one of the founders of the company I had been helping out. He hadn't come to me for help in a while so I asked him how their marketing was going. He told my they had hired a marketing expert from a big agency. This expert worked his day job and then came at night to help them out. I had not yet met him because I always rushed home from work to take care of my son. As Marcos was telling me about him, my boss passed by and said he wanted me to meet their new hire. "You guys can pick each other's brains on our marketing." Now part of me was happy for them, but the other part of me, my ego was like, "really?" Who is this guy and why would my boss want me to brainstorm with him for our marketing? Did he think this agency guy was better than me? I told my ego to calm down. I knew that brainstorming with bright people was good, but my ego kept poking at me. I was enjoying the Brazilian sausages and drinks when suddenly this guy came up to me out of nowhere and introduced himself. I looked at him and instantly felt a peace within– a calmness I had never experienced before. He then told me he was the one doing marketing for the company I had been helping out. So, he was my "competition." Somehow, now that he was in front of me, the last thing I thought of was work and my ego took the back door. All I wanted to do was get to know him better. Marcos came around and served us some Caipirinhas that he had made and was proud of. Hot Agency Guy (that was the name I gave him) and I toasted our meeting. I was hooked – we started talking about everything. I told him about my coaching and my son. He told me about his work and the things he loved. As we talked, we realized that besides working in the same building, his best friend was my mentor at Toastmasters. We couldn't believe it. What a small world. Funny thing is that the day before, I had liked a picture of my mentor on Facebook. He was working out at the gym with a guy I didn't know. When I liked the picture, it was if an electric shock went through my body. I could not understand it. I "unliked" the picture and then liked it again. Once again, the same kind of shock went through me. Now Hot Agency Guy took out his phone and showed me the Facebook picture. He was the one who had been working out in the gym with my mentor. What

Divine synchronicity. We were so happy over our close common connections that we just hugged in the middle of the terrace in front of everyone. It felt like the most natural thing in the world.

Two girls arrived and he excused himself to go talk to them. Great, he has a girlfriend. What was I thinking? I went off to talk with someone else. Then he came around and introduced the girls to me. I got quite a look from one of them; I wasn't sure what exactly was going on. I went on to talk to others at the barbecue. The next thing I knew, the Hot Agency Guy was beside me again and the girls had left. He told me they were his friends and had stopped by to see him. I later found out one of the girls had been interested in him and was hoping to spend time with him at the party but when he didn't show any interest, they left early. Apparently, the girl told him sarcastically: "You will end up hooking up with her" referring to me. Lucky me.

We continued our conversation and laughed a lot. He took my hand and pretended he knew how to read palms, making up all kinds of crazy stuff. He was fun, interesting, sociable and did I mention this? Hot! Although I was tired and had to wake up for work the next morning, I didn't want the night to end. But, I did the sensible thing and told him I had to leave. He walked me to my car and we hugged. I did not want to leave his arms. He felt so good. He felt so warm. I felt like I knew him forever. As he was hugging me, I asked the Universe, is he THE ONE? He gave me a small kiss beside the mouth. I felt this was a nice touch. I smiled. I loved it. He said, "I'll let you go home now." I replied: "No, I want to stay with you." Then he really kissed me. It was so amazing. It was so beautiful.   It was magical. I felt a bit uncomfortable because I didn't want any co-workers to see, not to mention the fact that my car was parked in front of a mosque. I could imagine what the people in there would think about kissing in public. All these fears popped into my head. I pushed those fears aside and enjoyed the kissing. How could it get even better than this?

COACHING TIP: When you least expect it, magic happens. Expect it ☺

Chapter 15

WTF?

I woke up the next day feeling I was walking on clouds. What an amazing guy I had just met. He ended the night by saying, "I would like one day to wake up with you and make you pancakes." What a beautiful good bye. Wake up and make me pancakes. I started to dream about it. What a man and what kind of pancakes would he make? 😊 Over the next two months Hot Agency Guy and I saw each other quite regularly. It was so amazing. It was so much fun. I felt he really got me. He was smart, he was deep, he was spiritual and he was funny. We had the exact same type of high energy as well as drive for personal growth and success. Once, Hot Agency Guy came over when my son was home. My son took an instant liking to him and he is not the type that takes an instant liking to just anyone. They played a bit, they talked and when I told my son he had to go to bed, tears welled up in his eyes. He wanted to stay with us longer. I had never seen my son react to anyone like this before. He was close to his grand-parents, friends, my friends, yet he never had tears in his eyes to say good bye to someone. I was touched. I believe children sense people as they really are better than adults. My son is quite intuitive.

Hot Agency Guy and I enjoyed shopping for groceries and cooking together. What a chef; I must admit he was a better cook than me. He just did not cease to impress me. We both had a love for hiking, biking, traveling and a thirst for becoming our best selves in every way. I often felt this was too good to be true.

I will never forget that Tuesday in September. In the morning we were planning a trip to California together but in the afternoon, whoops, I got "The Call." He started by saying he couldn't make the trip to California and then he said he wouldn't be able to see me on Thursday. Then he went on to say he was busy looking for a new apartment and sub-leasing his so he wasn't sure when he could see me again. I was reeling with shock. What was happening? What changed from morning till now? I asked him if I had done anything to upset him and he said no. I told him his behavior was not like him and kept asking questions. And then I asked the big question: "Is there someone else?" He replied that one of his ex-girlfriends had gone to see him and they decided to give their relationship another shot. WTF? This did not feel right. Out of nowhere he decides to go back to an ex-girlfriend? It seemed out of context. We hung up and I was in total disbelief. How could this have happened? Why would the Universe put me in this position? Why would I meet someone so amazing only to have him dump me? Things just weren't adding up. I was angry, I was hurt, I was confused. All I wanted to do was cry. What Universal lesson could there possibly be in all of this because it just felt so wrong? That there were no good men out there? That when it seems too good to be true, it is? Had I been played? Had I been manipulated? The questions and disbelief were endless. I kept on asking... why is this happening to me?

My friends were also in disbelief. They all agreed it did not add up and assured me he would come around. One of my dear coaching friends, Christine Lecavalier, told me: "It's not happening TO you, it's happening FOR you." What? How was this happening FOR me?

The Universe works in mysterious ways. Out of the blue, our bosses set us up in a meeting together to discuss marketing strategies. What a meeting. I had to keep a straight professional face. I kept looking at him and thinking, "…you were in my home, you met my son, you know so much of me and now you are sitting in a meeting beside me, completely cold." I put my best marketing face forward remaining as professional as I could in front of everyone. He was completely dry. I left the meeting completely drained and decided to go take out my pain and frustrations at the gym. When I finished my workout, I realized he had texted me saying: "It was nice seeing you. You brought up some really good ideas at the meeting." What? This man was making me crazy. I did not want to be in the same situation that I had been in my previous breakup.

I contacted my Shaman and asked him to cut the energetic cords between me and this man. I did not want to cry anymore; I did not want to suffer. He told me that by breaking the cords, it cuts everything that did not work between you two." So if it's meant for you two to get back together, it will be a fresh new beginning. The energetic vibes that did not work before will no longer be present." Funny how everyone was feeling there was a possibility of us getting back together. John cut the cords between us and I started to feel some heaviness lifted from me.

Hot Agency Guy and I kept bumping into each other at work. We bumped into each other at a few events at which we did not know the other had been invited. It seems we were bumping into each other a lot. At all these events, he was nice to me. He was treating me as if we were still together. I just didn't get it. I had to go to California to see my newly hired business coach. I had signed up with an elite coach for a one-year Mastermind program. I chose her because I felt we had a similar path. She also had a background in marketing, she had also been a single mom, and now she had a coaching business, making millions. I felt she could help me speed up my business growth. I went to San Diego and re-charged. I met some fantastic people, got some great business ideas to boost my sales and enjoyed soaking my feet in the sand even though it was only for a few minutes. I was happy to have signed up to this program. There was so much for me to learn as an entrepreneur.

Every time I meditated and asked questions about Hot Agency Guy, the Universe kept on telling me: "Love him. Trust. He is the one. You are together." I didn't understand. We obviously weren't physically together. What kind of games was the Universe playing on me?

I came back from San Diego and bumped into him again. He asked if we could talk. I agreed. I was so excited to see him again. We went for sushi, we had some tea, and we went for a beautiful walk on Mont Royal. It was as if we had never been apart. After the beautiful evening, I asked, "So what about your girlfriend?" He paused for a long time and said: "I am going to tell you something, but you have to swear to me you will never repeat it. You repeating it can cost me my job." Cost him his job? What? I assured him I would not repeat it. He looked at me deep in the eyes and said, "It's your ex-husband; I know him." WTF? How do you know him? How is that possible? He looked at me, hesitated and then said, "He's my CEO." Whaaat? How could that be? My son's dad worked in an insurance company and Hot Agency Guy worked in marketing. He then said my first husband's name and added: "He's my CEO." I was in total shock.

I had not told him I had been married twice. I was so ashamed; I felt like a failure for having had two divorces. But I had no choice than to be honest now. I told him that his CEO was not my son's dad. "I was married before; your CEO is my first husband." I expected him to look at me with disgust and hate me forever. Why would he be attracted to someone who was twice divorced? He looked at me with the biggest smile and laughed. What a relief!

The mood lightened somewhat as he then went on to tell me the story. He and his CEO were on LinkedIn for work purposes and my name showed up under the search they were doing. His CEO saw that he and I were connected on LinkedIn and said: "That is my ex-wife." Hot Agency Guy was shocked and uncomfortable. His CEO had spoken about his ex-wife before but he had no idea it was me. Hot Agency Guy was afraid he'd lose his job if his CEO found out we were dating so that's why he broke up with me so suddenly. When he found out his CEO was not my son's dad, he was relieved. He had been afraid my son would say something to his dad and he didn't want his CEO to find out at any cost. Well, at least now I had my answers. Now it made sense. I was relieved and happy to know. So my intuition was not off. What were the chances that of all the people in the world, his CEO had to be my first husband? What was the message here? We are all connected in some way. We ended the night with a hug and agreed to meet again. We didn't talk about getting back together, just about seeing each other again. Hot Agency Guy still feared his CEO, although less so now that he knew the CEO was Husband #1.

When I went home that night I asked myself what did I have to learn from this? TRUST. When you feel that something or someone is right for you, trust that if it's meant for you, it will come to you. I did feel he was meant for me. When I doubted that, I would remind myself of the tears in my son's eyes. There was a reason for that. So how was this situation happening FOR me? Was it so I could finally come out of the closet and admit I was twice divorced? Was it for me to see that he loved me for who I was regardless of my past? Was it for us to appreciate our relationship more? Was it for me to realize I had to work on loving all of me, the good, the bad, and my past, as all of this is what makes me, me? I believe it was all of the above. I went back to see John Chu for some more hypnosis to help me get rid of my subconscious fears. I knew the only way to change an end result was to change the way I thought and felt. Hypnosis was a great way to remove subconscious blockages that were preventing me from moving forward.

COACHING TIP: Trust that if something is meant for you, it will come to you.

Chapter 16

To Listen or Not to Listen?

Hot Agency Guy and I were officially back together again. I was happy to be back with my love. It was comforting. Now I had the fuel to focus more on my coaching business. My aim was to get as many clients as possible so I would have enough income to comfortably leave my marketing position. After all, I was a single mom; and needed to ensure as smooth a transition as possible. The business coach I hired in California had told me to "jump and the net will follow." Meaning, don't worry if you don't have the clients now, jump and the money will come. I found this risky considering my situation. But her voice was always in the back of my mind. I was learning so much from this coach and her Mastermind program. She was a successful coach making millions per year with clients around the world. She told me she would give me the tools to attract more clients and I was a good and eager student.

I had years of experience working in sales, marketing and business development for a range of companies, from large multinationals to small startups. I knew my stuff but I had never run my own business. And I had certainly never sold myself the way entrepreneurs need to do. So I listened to everything she said. I followed every bit of advice she gave me, to the letter. She provided me with templates about how I should write my marketing content, how I should conduct my webinars and how I should sell my coaching packages. She gave me her "formulas." The techniques and strategies she taught me were the very same ones that had helped her achieve success.

Strangely, they felt wrong for me. When I followed her marketing advice, the content I produced lacked authenticity. It wasn't my voice and it definitely wasn't an expression of my true self. On top of that, I wasn't getting results. When I told my coach this, she counseled me to be consistent and eventually, the results would come. They didn't.

That was my first red flag. Yet, seeing as how she was who she was, I chose to continue to follow her advice, even though I felt terrible and my inner voice was screaming at me to STOP. In addition to marketing, I also followed her advice on selling coaching packages. Her process involved bringing people's fears forward and insisting they pay for a package on the spot. That meant that she would ask for a client's credit card information during her first conversation with a potential client. It wasn't for a small amount, it was for thousands of dollars. Her rationale was that people come to coaches for help, so it was our obligation as coaches to do what we believed was best for them, and to pressure them into a sale before they changed their minds.

Hmmm, this felt oddly like my experience with the relationship coaching package I bought. Templates, no powerful questions, packages and no refunds... I didn't like it when I was the one buying these, why would I sell this way? Her technique wasn't necessarily wrong... for her... but it felt wrong to me. Another red flag.

I listened to her, even though my gut was telling me

not to. And it didn't work. I didn't sell a single package that way. I finally stopped listening to what felt wrong. I started listening to what felt right. I chose to be brave; to listen to my own instincts and forge my own path. I must admit, it was difficult and scary but I couldn't ignore the loud voice inside of me. I developed marketing and sales strategies that aligned with my core values.

Here's an example: When it came to selling, instead of asking for credit card information on the first conversation, I started giving people time between our conversations to think about my packages and services to let them decide if working with me felt right for them. That's when I started selling. My feeling was that if someone was meant to work with me, it would happen; I didn't want my clients to make decisions based on fear. That's not how I coach people in making decisions, so I certainly didn't want that to be the start of our coaching relationship. I want clients to make decisions from their hearts. When I think back to the coaches who made me pay upfront on the spot, I get a knot in my stomach. They left a sour taste in my mouth. They were big amounts; we are talking over $10K. They are probably selling more than me but I chose to put my values before my sales.

The result? People started signing up and came into the program ready and excited about the commitment they had just made. By listening to someone else's "formulas", by doubting myself and not listening to my inner voice, I had made a terrible mistake – one which had set me back in my progress and had caused me considerable discouragement.

I consider it my greatest failure as an entrepreneur – but also my greatest lesson. That failure taught me that just because a technique or strategy works successfully and results in millions of dollars for one person, it didn't mean that it was right for me. It taught me that the voice I needed to listen to first and foremost was the voice inside me. I needed to give that voice a megaphone. That inner voice, whatever you want to call it – instinct, gut feeling, intuition – knows your inner truth and passion. It knows your life's purpose; it knows what you have to do, even if you haven't figured it out yet. Now I coach others in finding their own voices, understanding their core values, their life's purpose, and creating strategies to align with their life and businesses. I help people bring meaning to everything they do, in all aspects of their lives. It's what I truly feel I was meant to do, and the joy I feel from living and working with authenticity is like no other.

COACHING TIP: Listen to your gut – your inner voice – it knows you best. And it, more than anyone, has your best interests at heart. And, it will never steer you wrong.

Chapter 17

Bye-Bye Boss &
Hello CEO of Myself

My coaching business was going well. I wanted to make it my full-time career but wasn't making enough money yet to justify it. It was a Catch-22 situation. I needed more time for marketing, but my days were consumed with my job, my son, my boyfriend and my current coaching clients. How could I stretch the days? Either I had to take the leap and quit my job trusting that the clients would come or be content with the current pace of building my practice. I felt I was bringing my best self forward in my coaching. I saw the transformations my clients were having and it felt so rewarding. I saw some clients triple their salaries, I saw many start businesses they love. I saw clients truly connecting to who they were and take brave steps to putting their true selves out in the world. It was so amazing. I HAD to do this all day long!

I was struggling with the big question: do I take the risk and leave my marketing job and pray that it will all work out? Or do I play it safe and keep the day job until I had a good nest egg on the side? I remember my coach telling me: "Always make decisions from where you want to be and not from where you are at." If I looked at the situation I was at, it was not a good decision to make the leap. If I looked at where I wanted to be – a coach making six-digits a year – then leaving my job was the next step. Leaving my job would open space for more time to market myself and attract more clients.

Now I assure you, this was by no means an easy decision. In fact, it was utterly terrifying. This monumental decision meant ignoring the reality of my bank account and having constant knots in my stomach. The voices of fear and doubt reared their ugly heads again. What if my business was not successful? What if I was unable to pay the mortgage? What if I could not support myself and my son? What if I had to move back in with my parents? I pushed those voices aside and forced myself to think new thoughts like; what if I succeed? What would that look like? I could work the hours I want. I could organize my schedule around my son's schedule to have more quality time with him. I could do what I loved all day long and inspire others to do the same. I had my vision of where I wanted to be, and it was very clear in my mind. I knew I had to take the leap. The question was when? I asked the Universe to guide me.

I went into work the next day and my boss pissed me off more than ever. Don't get me wrong, we still considered each other as friends. It's just that he kept asking me to re-do things I did not agree with. He had asked me to re-do the home page and messaging of the company website and I didn't agree with the direction he was taking. Normally, I would state my point and then go for what he wanted because after all, he was the boss. But this time I said no. I told him I didn't agree with this and wouldn't do it. He looked at me and said that his way was what he felt was best. I just couldn't take it anymore. I felt my credibility was being undermined. I wondered why did he need a vice president of marketing – if he just wanted someone to tell them what to do and listen to him, then what he needed was a marketing coordinator. I felt my skills weren't being used or appreciated. My Future Self was nudging me to say, "I quit." My gremlins were telling me..., "no...are you crazy?" In the midst of it all, I felt this was the Universe's way of saying "time to move on Melissa. You're ready." I took a deep breath. I gathered all my courage, I looked at my boss in the eyes and I said the two best words I could have said: "I quit." He looked at me in disbelief. "Come on Melissa," he said. I told him I was serious. "I don't feel I am contributing value here – you need an assistant that does what you say, not a vice president of marketing". He tried to convince me to stay but with those two words out there, I knew it was the right thing for me to do at this time.

I was scared, but it felt right. I called my boyfriend in a bit of disbelief. He was surprised but told me I did the right thing. It was comforting for someone to validate that I wasn't crazy. I went home that night happy – proud of myself I knew I would find my way as an entrepreneur and I would make my six-digit coaching business happen. I mean, so many others had done it, why not me?

COACHING TIPS: Always make decisions from Future You, from where you want to be, and not from where you are.

Chapter 18

Bringing the Best Version of You Forward

Finding the perfect relationship is not the answer to your problems, but that's the way I saw it through this period of my life.

Relationships are a mirror to the self and through our relationships we can learn vital lessons. They show us what we need to work on and teach us what makes us tick. When we get the feeling that a relationship we're in is no longer making us happy we are propelled to a higher path. It's healthy to let go of what no longer serves us, even other people if need be. That is how we grow and become better at being ourselves.

I always thought that the answer to all my problems and the object of my happiness would be found in a man. That is just so wrong! The answers to our deepest questions, our deepest desires and our quest for happiness is not in another person. I didn't know that years ago but now I know for sure; the answer is to first fall in love with yourself, nurture yourself, work on your personal growth and nourish your soul. The right relationship, the right man or woman for you is on the other side of self-work. Take care of yourself and you'll emit a positive vibration that will attract people at a higher vibration to you.

A relationship is healthy when you feel good, when you feel you can be yourself. If you don't, please move on so you can open yourself up to relationships and opportunities that will.

I promised myself I would continuously work on being the best version of myself, that I would shine my brightest light so that I could attract the best people, opportunities and clients. I do this by continuing to invest in my own personal growth and always choosing to see what I can learn, the gift in every situation that is taking me towards my next step forward.

Taking the leap into entrepreneurship has been an extremely exciting journey. As you can see it wasn't all lollipops and roses, there were some very tough times but I can honestly say, that's what makes the journey even sweeter.

Some months I earned three to four times my VP Marketing salary and other months I only took in half of it. The months I made half of it, were quite stressful. The gremlins would kick in. I learned to look at sales on a quarterly basis instead of a monthly basis. Would I recommend someone do what I did? It depends. The question you need to ask yourself is: "How much risk am I willing to live with?" If you are willing to lose everything for something you believe in, then I say go for it. If you feel you need certain stability, then ensure you either have a few months' savings on the side or some type of stable income either from a spouse or a part-time job.

I had a lot of fears but every time these fears came up, these are the five things I told myself to keep going – to try to get comfortable with the uncomfortable (the uncomfortable being a single mom with no stable paycheck):

1) What is the worst-case scenario of taking this leap and leaving my job? I lose my home? I know I can get another job at the snap of my fingers if things start to look bad. I owe it to myself to take that risk – to step into my full potential and make what I truly want happen.

2) Do not give in to panic. Do not allow your fears to lead you. Make decisions from the direction you are moving towards and not from where you are.

3) When you work for someone else, you are building their dream, their brand. Why not build your own dream, your own brand? No one can take this away from you. A job can be lost at any time and then what do you have left? When you build your own brand, it's yours forever; you can just keep building and creating.

4) I want to be an example for my child. I want to show him, through my own life and actions that he needs (and can) do what makes him feel alive. I want to show him that you need to do work that fulfills you and not be handcuffed to a day job you don't feel excited about.

5) I remember the quote saying that "97 per cent of the people who quit chasing their dreams are hired by the three per cent that didn't." I am determined to be the three percent.

What was the result of setting aside the position I was in and choosing instead to make such a huge decision from the mindset of where I wanted to be? By taking that huge leap, by choosing to go for what I truly wanted, I was able to replace my VP salary within half a year.

In less than six months, I was living a completely new reality – the reality I had dreamed for myself! I was living my life, my way. I was running a full-time business doing what I absolutely loved.

Today I coach other professionals and entrepreneurs how to bring their gifts forward into the world. And I have an amazing man who believes in me even when I doubt myself. He always encourages me to bring my best self forward in everything I do. The truth is, when you choose to invest in your personal growth, when you choose to work on healing, on what is going on in the inside of you, it will manifest on the outside. I spent months and years with coaches, therapists, hypnotists, Shamans and guides to heal the mysteries of what was in my inside. It is because of all this healing that I was able to create my big picture vision and move forward. And it doesn't end there. Healing and personal growth need to be continuous to keep taking your life, your relationships and your business to the next level. Keep going, don't stop.

DON'T GIVE UP

COACHING TIP: Never think it's too late to go for what you truly want, for what is important to you, for what sets your heart on fire. Through coaching, personal growth, healing, continuous steps, and your heart guiding you, you CAN make it happen. This is true whether it's the right partner, opportunity, or business.

Chapter 19

Interviews

I have shared my journey to show you what it took for me to attract an amazing partner and start a business that was meaningful to me with clients I loved working with. I have interviewed five people I highly respect to see what they felt it took for them to attract the right partner and clients they love. Each of these people is in a long-term happy relationship and each has a business with clients they love. I thought their journeys could also inspire yours.

These are the two questions I asked them:

- *What do you feel is needed to attract the right partner to you?*

- *What is needed to attract clients you love to you?*

Here are their responses:

**Rick Tamlyn - Thought Leader, Author -
Play Your Bigger Game, Keynote Speaker**

- *What do you feel is needed to attract the right partner to you?*

- *What is needed to attract clients you love to you?*

Both are the same question to me. Both are about love and intimacy. Philosophy is the same although context is different.

We are giving off energy all the time. We have an emotional impact in the space around us. We are literally vibrating. We are impacting space and space responds accordingly. The law of attraction is confirming how science works. I see into my world and find what I am looking for. Based on my level of consciousness, I will find my reality. We are always trying to make right decisions. If we do so based upon our passion and love, then we will find what is right and make it right. The right decision doesn't come from the decision but after the decision is made. We make things based on our perception of how we see them.

Based on what do I see first? Attraction has a flavor out there; we are more powerful at the equation. I am attracting it because I am looking for it.

When we come from a deficient space, we look outside to fulfill us. The Universe knows that and doesn't work that way. When you are coming from deficiency, it's a true core belief. It's the true sense of self which is the sense of the attraction. There are days which are gray and that doubt is the primary sense of self. I can put it in a pretty bow and put words around it, but if I really don't believe that, then you will get mirrored that back.

You need to realize when you are in deficiency. No matter how many affirmations you do, sometimes you need a good therapist. We cannot do it alone. A coach, a therapist that holds us in a different space – that is important.

Studying Carl Jung, The Self, what is my sense of self?

Do I feel safe, created, connected? Do I have a sense of

why I am here? It doesn't mean being happy and fulfilled all the time. Our sense of self is key to the attraction concept. A day of gray or blue doesn't mean I will attract the negative. It takes some time. If I can know that I am blue and gray and love myself in the midst of being blue and gray, then the Universe feels that love. This is the primary context of what is going on. What is the sense of Self? This is the source of what we attract and bring into our lives.

Humans have found different ways to get to the sense of Self. I want a sense of Self. I am okay. I am creative. I feel in harmony with my world. This sense of Self – as a nation, as a whole, each and every one of us – had been closeted and now society is opening up more and we have permission for it to come out. We are always co-creating. I am always co-creating the world around me. I am a part of all that happens. My mind impacts conversations.

There are different components to the sense of Self: passion and purpose, what lights me up? This is where love and intimacy come from. It's an act of love to put our passion into the world. What is my passion, what is my purpose? This is what matters to me.

You've got to show up. It's a doing and a being. What is the messaging? Your mess becomes your message. Whatever you are putting out there is the message you are giving others about yourself.

The right people will read it. The people who respond are the right people. Go from sense of self instead of what is needed out there.

It's all made up. If I believe it works like this, then it

does, the Universe mirrors it. Religion came up with stuff and decided how it happened. People who created religion decided how people should be controlled. Now we get to decide how we think it all works.

Hugh Culver
Keynote Speaker, Productivity expert, Author, Coach

- *What do you feel is needed to attract the right partner to you?*
- *What is needed to attract clients you love to you?*

Partner: I don't make you what you are, I make up how I see you. Curiosity comes from curiosity. Park your ego. Really be curious. Remember that you are looking for someone who has been on earth 20-plus years – it's about more than just good looks. Even when you are pissed off, be curious…what are they teaching you now? It's hard work. This is the work that it takes. It's easy to get mad, sad, frustrated anyone can do that – what is hard is to go into curiosity.

Client: In the Speaking world, the way to get clients you love, is by being a really, really good speaker –. to be so good they will find you more clients. These days especially because there is so much free information on social media, you need to be an authority. It's not good enough to know who else can do the job if you can't do it. Who else does your ideal client need? Be the authority. If they need help with their car, find it for them. Spend time every week to learn, attend conferences – be the expert in your field. That's why people come to you. You don't have to be a world expert, just resourceful. It comes down to developing a relationship, it's not just about the work – there should be real respect. When people call me for a favor, I will say yes first. I won't think about it. I will do whatever I can to make it work. With some clients, I have never raised my rates because I just feel the relationship is so good. They keep booking me.

John Germain Leto
Life, Soul & Image Coach, Author & Speaker

- *What do you feel is needed to attract the right partner to you?*

The coaching I received after my own breakup to a woman I thought I was supposed to marry brought me deeper into my personal inquiry: Stop seeking the right partner, instead become the right partner. For me, what I strive for each day as part of my vows, and what I also told my wife on our first date, is: "I must be the man that is worthy of your choosing, with the emphasis on "I must be".

I realize most people are seeking the right partner, spending more time on the partner aspect instead of time on themselves. They are both important. It's human nature to look outside ourselves instead of within. I meant it and still mean it each day. Now I have been married five years. Each day I can wake up and say, "Who is this man that is worthy of his ideal partner's choosing?" I presence it daily. In addition, two months before meeting my wife, I sat down and wrote out the woman I am grateful for as if she was in my life already. I listed everything from hair color, eye color, spiritual qualities, even cup size, all different things on every level.

There are four levels people can connect on: physical, mental, emotional, and energetic/spiritual. She is the first woman that I connected with on all four levels. I've had the good fortune to date many extraordinary women. Yet there was always something missing on at least one level. Even the woman I was engaged to before my wife, we connected on every level except mentally.

Keep the attention on yourself, "Who is the person that is worthy of his/her ideal partner's choosing?" We all want the full package. Keep in mind that people that have the full package have a lot of options. There is the surface level and a deeper level. I sat in uncertainty for a year before my wife committed to me. At that time, my journey was all about self-love. Through every trial, I kept asking myself, "What does a man of self-love do with this?" Someone needs to take this and internalize it for themselves. How does this sync up with a deeper emotional journey? It's not easy, it's always changing. We are always changing and evolving as people. Also, it's not only who you are, but who you are becoming. The partner that you are with, who we they becoming, and how is that compatible?

- What is needed to attract clients you love?

A client whose soul journey mirrors your own. With most clients that I enjoy, there is some aspect of their soul's journey that is mirrored in my own. I also have a vested interest in the things they are facing. A recent client that literally love had a heart attack before he started working with me because he wasn't listening to messages of his heart. He was working mostly from the level of the mind. He had to start to open his heart and allow it to lead the way in life and business. "What does that look like to be in inquiry of conscious flow? This applies to relationships with women and men, business opportunities and a relationship with oneself. This mirrors so much of my own journey. Also, something that I often say to the coaches that I coach is that you don't have to have it ALL figured out. You just need to be a few steps ahead to coach someone successfully. On the journey of the heart and soul, the coaching, energetic experiences, and mediations I facilitate are effortless. I have been in my own inquiry over the last four or five years of not forcing and being in a flow state. It's aligning with that flow that allows the highest wisdom to pour forth. It's also important that we each continue to do our own personal work.

Another aspect of what is needed to attract clients that you love is Resonance, the energetic undercurrent. Most people don't know what putting their heart into their business means. They think they know, but they really don't. This is what it means to me: You have to love it, every aspect of what you are doing. Love the inquiry. It's not something you have to try to do. How much do you have to try to love the person that you love? You don't have to get psyched up to love them. You just love them. It's a matter of choosing. You are choosing the focus of your work. When you choose things that align with your deepest gifts, it brings out your golden light. It calls you forth. I can express things from my heart in an open and honest way that is not taxing to me. It's effortlessly standing in your own strength and truth for the highest good of the other (the client).

Rick Carson
Author of Taming Your Gremlin® and A Master Class in Gremlin Taming ®

- *What do you feel is needed to attract the right partner to you?*
- *What is needed to attract clients you love to you?*

"In order for people to be drawn to you, they have to have an unabashed experience of who you really are—the natural you. The essence of the natural you have had many names. I've often called it true love. No description of the experience of true love can do justice to its glory. True love is both subtly and powerfully perfect. Just as the sun is always shining whether you can see it or not, true love exists within you always, whether or not you are attentive to it.

When true love comes into your awareness, it permeates your experience and you feel content, peaceful and satisfied. When you allow your voice, your words, your facial expressions and your actions to reflect this true love, people are attracted to you.

Experiencing true love does not require something or someone to love—though you may feel true love inside yourself in the presence of certain people and things. Nor do you ensure yourself a large dose of true love by smiling a lot, talking softly, or hugging people with whom you'd just rather shake hands and say "howdy".

The experience of true love differs from the experience of excitement, sexual feeling, adoration, or desire, though these pleasurable sensations increase in lip-smacking intensity when laced with or founded upon true love. Pleasurable stimulation can be thrilling; ask your taste buds or your genitals. But even a first-class titillating tingle remains only pleasurable stimulation until you are awakened to the experience of true love lying in a half-sleep behind your heart. Add to that pleasurable stimulation one small full-bodied drop of pure love, and you're in for a real treat. Tapping into that true love and thus into the natural you is the essence of attraction and what Taming Your Gremlin® is all about.

Diana Eskander
Love Coach with a conscious approach

- *What do you feel is needed to attract the right partner to you?*

- *What is needed to attract clients you love to you?*

Meeting the right partner begins with your mindset and your beliefs. What you believe to be true about love, people, yourself and relationships will continue to show up in your reality. Getting clear on what your beliefs are gives you the opportunity to shift the ones that don't serve you. Infused in this process is a massive dose of self-love. When your cup is full with your own love and you're not thirsty for it, you become the curator of your relationships. It's important to realize that you cannot share with someone what you don't have. If you want to share love, you've got to have love. That begins with giving it to yourself! Relationships serve as mirrors of your internal landscape, so whatever you're lacking in the relationship with yourself will show up in those you have with others. Self-love and authenticity set the foundation for true connections. When you're in a positive space and you've learned how to fulfill your own needs, you can start getting specific about what you want in your next love experience - your relationship vision. This is something I help my clients create because the relationship vision, whether you're single or in a relationship, serves as a roadmap for how to live your life. Are you a match to your ideal partner and relationship vision? If you want to be with someone who is joyous, confident and authentic, ask yourself, am I being all those things myself? Be the type of person you want to be in a relationship with and do the things you want to do with them. Not only is this valid in a practical sense, because you're more likely to meet people who have similar interests, but also from a vibrational level — you need to match the vibration of that which you want. If you want to find your soul mate, you need to mate with your soul!

Clients

This is similar for attracting the right clients. You have to be in the essence of the type of people you wish to work with. For example, if you want to work with clients who are engaged, receptive and respectful, you need to exude those qualities in everything that you do. It's the law of attraction: like attracts like. This is how we build our tribes and our inner circles. We can have differences and in fact, the contrast is what keeps things interesting — the important thing is to align with your values.

Coaching Tips
from
I Attract What I Am

- Always listen to your inner voice – especially when it's screaming. If you ignore that voice, the Universe will challenge you with harder and harder trials until you start listening.

- When something or someone you want is a constant struggle to get, it's the Universe telling you it's not meant for you.

- When you hit rock bottom and you consciously decide to make changes that feel good, the Universe supports you by propelling you forward.

- Need to make a tough decision? Ask yourself, "What would "the me" of my ideal future decide?" When you want something to be different in life, you have to be ready to do something different.

- Do not listen to what the "experts" tell you. If something feels wrong, it probably is. Always trust your inner voice.

- Never ever ignore the red flags. They're put there for you as signs from the Universe.

- No matter how bad things seem, remember things are happening FOR you and not TO you.

- The Universe truly does have your back. Trust that when

one door closes, it's a sign that a new and better one is waiting to open for you.

- Move towards everything that brings your soul pure child-like joy. That is your path.

- When we go with the flow of life instead of our fixed vision, we open up to something bigger than we could have ever imagined.

- In everything you do, always start with an internal analysis; always start with you. Ask yourself what you truly want and what you want to create based on what fuels you, your values and your life purpose.

- To get different results, you need to do something different.

- There are good coaches and there are not-so-good coaches. Everyone resonates with different people. You can learn from even a bad coach. You can learn what you don't want so moving forward; you are more aware of what you do want.

- When looking for a coach, look for one who is where you want to be and that is aligned with your values.

- Whenever you are in a situation you are not happy with, ask yourself: "What did I learn from this?"

- Trust in Divine timing. Things will happen when they are meant to happen. The Universe has your back. Trust. And, don't worry about how.

- When you least expect it, magic happens. Expect it :-)

- Trust that if something is meant for you, it will come to you.

- Listen to your gut – your inner voice – it knows you best. And it, more than anyone, has your best interests at heart. And, it will never steer you wrong.

- Always make decisions from Future You, from where you want to be, and not from where you are.

- Never think it's too late to go for what you truly want, for what is important to you, for what sets your heart on fire. Through coaching, personal growth, healing, continuous steps, and your heart guiding you, you CAN make it happen. That is true whether it's the right partner, opportunity, or business.

Free Resources

Six Steps Towards Determining Your Core Values So You Never Have to Struggle with Them Again

You will get exercises and tips to:
- Determine your core values
- Provide you with direction and clarity
- Be true to who you really are
- https://ceoofyour.life/values/

10 Steps Towards Creating the Orgasmically Joyful Life & Career You Really Crave

You will get exercises and tips that will help you:
- Combine your passion and your career
- Remove obstacles to living the life you love
- Uncover your unique gifts
- http://melissadawn.ca/ebook.php

Nine Steps for an Orgasmically Joyful Life & Business

You will receive powerful and actionable exercises and tips to:
- Create your ideal vision for the life and business you truly want and deserve
- Overcome and eliminate the roadblocks preventing you from moving forward
- Stay on track, continuously course correct and sail towards your targets
- https://ceoofyour.life/ebook/

Acknowledgments

I would like to thank my amazing life and business partner. It is the first time that I feel loved for being truly me. I want to thank him for believing in me even before I believed in myself. His belief in me as I am gave me the confidence that propelled me forward. His support day in and day out contributed greatly towards me creating my orgasmically joyful life and business. My gratitude to him goes beyond what words can say. It is deep. It is truly heartfelt. It is priceless.

I am so grateful to my son. He does not realize the important role he has played in my life. Let's face it, life has ups and downs. When things got really down, he was the reason I picked myself up. I wanted to be the best mom possible for him. I wanted to show him that no matter how tough things get, you can always turn them around. He is such a wise soul. He has taught me a lot and continues to do so.

I would like to thank all my teachers, coaches, and guides who helped me in every step in my journey and were there for me above and beyond their call of duty.

I would like to thank my friends and family who supported me in this journey, even when they thought what I was doing was crazy.

I am truly grateful to Carolyn Flower and her team for showing me the steps and supporting me in publishing my first book.

I would like to thank the Universe for sending me the people I needed when I needed them and for guiding and inspiring me with this book. Thank you, thank you, and thank you.

References

Professional Development Training

Access Consciousness® offers pragmatic tools to change things in your life that you haven't been able to change until now. www.accessconsciousness.com

Coaches Training Institute, CTI®, is the largest in-person coach training school in the world and the only program to teach CTI's ground-breaking Co-active Coaching® model in highly interactive courses. CTI's proven whole-life coaching approach enables people to achieve success and fulfillment in their work and life through a powerful coach/client alliance that promotes and enhances the lifelong process of learning. www.coactive.com

ThetaHealing® a meditation training technique utilizing a spiritual philosophy for improvement and evolvement of mind, body and spirit.

Book Reference

Walsch, N.D , (1995). Conversations with God - An Uncommon Dialogue - Book 1. New York, NY: G.P. Putnam's Sons

Biography

Melissa Dawn is Founder of CEO Of Your Life.

Melissa is a Certified Professional Life and Business Coach (CPCC), Motivational Speaker (Canadian Association of Professional Speakers – CAPS) and earned a Bachelor of Commerce (BComm). She's a regular contributor to the Huffington Post and Entrepreneur.com and has been featured on many podcasts including Entrepreneur on Fire, Breakfast Television, CJAD Radio, the Edmonton Journal, and more.

Melissa left behind a successful career as an award-winning V.P. in marketing to be of greater service. Her unique transformational process helps people to crystallize their vision to create a life that is a true reflection of who they are.

By adhering to the step-by-step guidance to become the CEO of their life, Melissa's clients gain power over who they are and what they do so they feel innately energized, inspired and powered-UP.

You too can become the CEO of your personal and professional life with confidence and success by engaging in and implementing the simple step-by-step strategies of her signature coaching programs.

Melissa is the Amazon international bestselling author of I Attract What I Am: Transform Failure into an Orgasmically Joyful Life and Business and is currently working on her second book.

Made in the USA
Middletown, DE
08 September 2019